S. NIRBERT

CONTENTS.

3

PREFACE

Unfortunately Saint Norbert and the Order he founded, the White Canons, are not nearly as well known today as they deserve to be. Yet he was one of the outstanding personalities in the Church during the first half of the 12th century and was recognized as such by his contemporaries who considered him to be at least the equal of his friend, the great Saint Bernard of Clairvaux. In the years immediately after his death there were many who wrote about him but none of them gave the whole story of his life. Therefore the need for a definitive biography became all the more urgent as those who had known the saint grew old and so the work was taken in hand in the mother abbey of Prémontré at the instance and under the direction of the Abbot General, Blessed Hugh of Fosses, who had been Saint Norbert's earliest disciple. All the monasteries which had been founded by the saint himself were asked to help and the information that they sent in was collated and, after careful revision, incorporated in the final text. The anonymous author, evidently a canon of Prémontré, says that everything that he wrote came from his own recollection as eyewitness of the events which he described or from the first hand accounts of other reliable eyewitnesses who were still alive, except for the earliest part of the story which was derived from what Saint Norbert himself had told him about his life before he left Xanten. This book, which must have been completed some time between 1155 and 1164, became the official life of the saint and copies were made for the other abbeys of the White Canons. It was a devotional work intended for spiritual reading in the monasteries of the Order and the narrative is filled out with an abundance of scriptural quotations and pious reflections. Basically, however, it is a trustworthy record of the facts, although regrettably it tells us nothing about Saint Norbert's achievements as a statesman and little of his immense service to the Church as one of the leading churchmen of his day, especially in the critical situation created by the schism of the anti-pope Anacletus II. But, as the author himself said, it was not possible for one man on his own to know or to find out everything.

Until 1856 this was the only contemporary biography known to scholars but in that year a 13th century manuscript, which had come from the monastery of Saint Peter at Brandenburg, was published in the «Monumenta Germaniae Historica». This life, which must have been written in one of the White Canons' monasteries in Saxony during the 12th century is much simpler and more direct in its style than the Prémontré life and is devoid of the pious reflections. It covers most of the same ground but its writer is more familiar with German places and people and is better informed about Saint Norbert's dealings with the Emperor Lothar III and about the expedition into Italy in 1132-33. Which of the two lives may have been the earlier and what was the relationship between them or whether they both drew on a still earlier life have been matters of dispute among scholars. What is certain, however, is that there are numerous passages in them that are worded identically and many others where one appears to be following the other. Roger Wilmans, who discovered the German life called it «Vita A», claiming that it was written first and was the source of the Prémontré life, generally known as «Blessed Hugh's life», which he named «Vita B».

Besides these two lives there are several other valuable early sources :

In his work on «**The Miracles of our Lady of Laon**», written in 1149, the monk Hermann of Laon devotes Book III to Bishop Bartholomew and includes an account of Saint Norbert and the foundation of Prémontré. He obtained his information from the Bishop and Blessed Hugh of Fosses, and possibly also from Saint Norbert himself.

«**The Chronicle of Sigebert of Gembloux**» was continued between 1140 and 1155 by a White Canon who records the events of Saint Norbert's life chronologically.

«**The Appendix of the Brethren of Kappenberg**» to the Prémontré life, which was sent to the mother abbey at Blessed Hugh's request, reproduces useful information about Saint Norbert's work in founding the Order taken from the «**Life of Godfrey of Kappenberg**».

«**The Chronicle of the Bishops of Magdeburg**» is a valuable contemporary source for Saint Norbert's life as archbishop.

Finally there is «**The Chronicle of Gottesgnaden**» which relates the history of the foundation of that monastery.

Such are the principal sources but it has been stated with truth that even if they had all been lost it would still have been possible to reconstruct the story of Saint Norbert's life from various chronicles and annals of the period as well as the numerous charters, deeds and papal bulls and the letters of Saint Bernard.

None of the sources gives the minute detail that is looked for in a modern biography but we do get a very clear and vivid picture of the personality of Saint Norbert and, whilst this book makes no pretence to be in any sense a learned work, its material has been drawn, wherever possible, directly from the original sources.

Before the invention of printing, copies of the life of Saint Norbert were only to be found in the monasteries of his Order but in 1572 the Carthusian Surius included it in a collection of the lives of Saints. However the text which he used was defective and in 1656 J.C. Van der Sterre, Abbot of Saint Michael's at Antwerp, published a scholarly edition of the Prémontré life (Vita B) after collating more than 16 of the oldest manuscripts from many different countries, giving the variant readings where these existed. This was reproduced in 1695 by Papebroch, one of the Bollandists, in their «Acta Sanctorum». Since that date many lives have appeared in different languages but the only lives in English were «The Life of Saint Norbert» by Rt. Rev. Abbot Geudens, O. Praem., (London 1886) and «The History of Saint Norbert» by Rev. Cornelius J. Kirkfleet, O. Praem., (Herder, St. Louis, U.S.A. 1916). Three of the best among the many lives in French, which have been immensely helpful in the writing of this book are «La Vie de Saint Norbert» by Rt. Rev. Louis Charles Hugo, O. Praem., Abbot of Etival, (Lille 1704), «Histoire de Saint Norbert», (3rd revised edition - Tongerlo 1928), by Rt. Rev. Godefroid Madelaine, O. Praem., of Mondaye, sometime Abbot of Frigolet, who had incidentally been confessor of Saint Theresa of Lisieux, and «Norbert et l'origine des Prémontrés» by Rev. François Petit, O. Praem., (Les Editions du Cerf - 1981). The first is a sound historical work written in a style of great clarity and beauty and made invaluable by the abundant notes that give the full text of a variety of original sources. Abbot Madelaine's book is the culmination of a lifetime's study and reflection, the earlier editions having appeared in 1886 and 1900, and gives a complete account of Saint Norbert's life and work drawn from the original sources, which are quoted throughout in the footnotes. Father Petit's work is likewise the fruit of a lifelong devotion and scholarship by a great authority on Saint Norbert and his Order. It is in a clear and lucid style and is eminently readable. It places the saint in the context of the movement of reform initiated by Saint Gregory VII and the opposition to it in the Church.

One of the most difficult problems encountered in writing this book has been to know how to deal with the lengthy accounts in the early lives of the activities of evil spirits; almost a quarter of Vita A is taken up by detailed narratives of diabolical possession and exorcism. Saint Norbert's contemporaries were always looking for tangible and visible evidence of the intervention of demons in human affairs, whereas today many doubt even the existence of evil spirits, although the Church has always taught a belief in the Devil and his angels who tempt men in all kinds of subtle ways. Many of the phenomena described in our sources are without any doubt attributable to psychic disorders or mental illness but there may well be a residue which is due to genuine demonic activity. Moreover it seems certain that there is often a causal connection between sin or moral evil and mental or even physical illness and it is worth noting that in several cases in which he performed an exorcism Saint Norbert explicitly stated that the possession was the consequence of the wrong doing of the person concerned. In all cases his primary purpose was to restore the reign of God in the soul by the power of Christ, exercised above all through the Mass, and often it is related that as a result the person was brought back to health of mind and body. The various manifestations of the Devil in which he sought by his attacks to deceive or disturb Saint Norbert need not surprise anyone who has read of similar events in the life of a modern saint, John Mary Vianney, the Curé d'Ars.

Finally it only remains to express my heartfelt thanks to all who have helped me. Without my wife and her constant help, advice and encouragement this book would never have been written. I have been greatly helped by the members of the community at Storrington, especially the late Prior Neill, O. Praem. and the present Prior, Rt. Rev. G. Joye, O. Praem., Rev. Fr. Andrew Smith, O. Praem., Rev. Fr. Ian MacLean, O. Praem., and Rev. Fr. Stephen Cannse, O. Praem., who very kindly translated from a work in Flemish for me. My special thanks are due to Rev. Fr. François Petit, who gave me a great deal of help and advice and whose work, especially «La Spiritualité des Prémontrés aux XIIe et XIIIe Siècles» has been most useful.

P.S. Since I wrote this book my wife has died. Please say a prayer for her.

INTRODUCTION.

Saint Norbert was German by birth, descended from the Salian Franks who inhabited the area of Brabant and Flanders which is today part of Belgium and the Southern Netherlands but then belonged to the Duchy of Lower Lorraine.

In the early Middle Ages the Kingdom of Germany was still the greatest and most powerful in Europe, enjoying a pre-eminence that had been built up by the Kings of the Saxon and Salian dynasties. From the beginning its rulers had been able to rely on the loyal support of the Church and in return had rewarded it generously with grants of lands and privileges.

By a strange irony it was the very success of the German monarchy that was to lead to its downfall. Otto the Great had revived the Empire when he had himself crowned as Emperor by Pope John XII in 962. This meant that he also became King of Italy, although his effective rule was restricted to the North of the peninsula. Had his successors been able to concentrate their efforts and resources on organizing and consolidating their German kingdom they might well have made it a strong, unified state that would have dominated the rest of Europe. Instead, following the will-o'-the-wisp of empire, they were frequently absent from Germany, dissipating their strength by military expeditions into Italy from which they got little profit, whilst the climate sapped their health and that of their armies. It was the Empire, too, that involved them in the long conflict with the Popes that was to prove fatal to them.

None of this could have been foreseen in the middle of the IIth century during the reign of Henry III (1039-1056). His position in Germany was secure, his rule in Italy was effective and his relations with the Church were excellent. He was a strong, capable and just ruler and a deeply religious man who had the best interests of his kingdom and of the Church at heart. Unfortunately he died in 1056, not yet forty years of age, leaving as his heir a child of six whose reign of fifty years (1056-1106) was to alternate between triumph and disaster.

The infant King, Henry IV, grew up to be a man of culture and artistic tastes but selfish and sensual; lacking in patience, he was prone to outbursts of passion and was a poor judge of character. Religion had no place in his life and he was an uncompromising opponent of the movement of reform in the Church, being notorious for his traffic in bishoprics and abbacies. His one ambition was to restore the power and prestige of the monarchy which had been eroded during his long minority. He meant, as Emperor, to make himself master of the Church with the Pope subordinate to him. In deliberate defiance of the Church's decrees, recently renewed by the Pope, he persisted in appointing bishops and abbots on his own authority. He thus embarked on a course that must bring him into conflict with the Pope, Saint Gregory VII (1073-1085), who even before his election, as Archdeacon Hildebrand, had been one of the foremost protagonists of reform in the Church. Gregory was a man of peace, who would gladly have worked in harmony with Henry, but he could not ignore such a flagrant challenge to the independence of the Church. So, when all his appeals and warnings were disregarded, he excommunicated the King and released his subjects from their allegiance to him. Being at this moment also in great danger from a rebellion in Germany Henry feigned repentance and to this day he is best remembered as the penitent standing barefoot in the snow outside the castle of Canossa. Absolved by the Pope he soon restored his authority in Germany and returned to his old ways. He even won the support of the German bishops and set up an anti-pope who crowned him as Emperor. Once again he was excommunicated and the civil war dragged on with varying fortunes until 1099 when, completely disheartened, he gave up the struggle and the nobles agreed to recognize his son as heir to the throne.

This son, Henry V (1106-1125), was ambitious, hard, ruthless and quite devoid of scruples. Like his father he was determined to restore the German monarchy to its former greatness and, seeing how it was now declining under his father, he made up his mind to get the royal power into his own hands as soon as possible, despite the oath he had taken never to act independently during the old King's lifetime. By 1104 he had succeeded in building up his own party amongst the nobles and in seducing his father's chief supporters and was posing as champion of the Church against the excommunicated King. When he was foiled by the loyalty of the Rhineland towns he persuaded his father to meet him and treacherously made him prisoner. The old King escaped and his son was twice defeated heavily by the nobles of Lorraine and the townsmen of the Rhineland, However he did not survive for long – he died, a broken man, in August 1106. In all the towns through which his body passed on the way to Spires, where it was to lie for years without christian burial, the citizens mourned sincerely for one who had always been their friend against the nobles.

The new king began his reign with several advantages that his father had lacked. He was already twenty five years of age and had been associated in the government of the kingdom for the past eight years, whilst he enjoyed the support of the Church. (1)

When Henry V came to the throne Norbert was in his early twenties.

(1) Henry V married Mathilda, daughter of Henry I of England. By her second marriage to Fulk, Count of Anjou, she was to be the mother of Henry II of England, the first king of the House of Plantagenet.

CHAPTER I

THE BACKGROUND AND EARLY YEARS.

About ten miles South of Nijmegen in the Netherlands, on a narrow tongue of land, where the River Niers flows into the Maas, there stands a tree-covered mound and a few fragments of masonry of uncertain date. Here, until it was destroyed by the French in 1710, stood for many centuries the castle of Gennep. In the 11th century it must have been a fortress of considerable importance for, protected by water on three sides, it commanded all movement along the Maas as well as the southern approaches to the great forest of Kettel and from it the rich and powerful family of the Lords of Gennep took their name. They also held the lordship of the town of Xanten, some twenty miles to the East, on the left bank of the Rhine, and it was there, according to an ancient tradition, that a son called Norbert was born to Heribert, Lord of Gennep, and his wife, Hedwig, in about 1081 or 1082. As there was an elder son, named Heribert after his father, from whom the later Counts of Gennep were to be descended, he was from his earliest years destined for the Church. This in no way implied a vocation as we understand it today for it was customary at this period to provide careers in the Church for the younger sons of the nobility. (2)

(2) For a discussion of the date and place of birth and the ancestry of Saint Norbert see Appendix «A».

Xanten takes its name from the saints (sancti), Roman soldiers who were martyred there in the 3rd century. By the 11th century it had attained the status of a municipality and a large church had been built over the tomb of the martyrs. In 1028 this became a collegiate church with a provost and a chapter of canons, which included not only priests but also deacons and subdeacons as well as an establishment of clerks in minor orders to assist in the maintenance of the church and the performance of the services.

As soon as Norbert was considered old enough to leave home, probably about the age of eight, he was made a member of the chapter and began his education. We know that there was a school attached to the church at Xanten and we may presume that it was here that he was entered as a pupil, although his more advanced studies must almost certainly have been made at one of the cathedral schools, which were then the great centres of learning.

Schooling in Northern Europe at this period was restricted almost exclusively to the clergy. All books were copied by hand on expensive parchments so that scholars did not read widely but studied a few books intensively. Moreover the language of the schools everywhere was Latin and their teaching was based on the surviving classical literature.

When Norbert went to school the course of studies was still the same as that followed in the last years of the Roman Empire and comprised the seven subjects of the **trivium** and the **quadrivium.** First came Grammar in which the principal authors studied were Cicero, Virgil and Ovid and the students had to practise Latin composition in both prose and verse. This was followed by Rhetoric, not so much to teach the art of public speaking as to instruct in writing, especially official correspondence.

The last subject in the **trivium** was Dialectic, a training in logic, based on Aristotle, although only two of his lesser works were known at this time. It was out of this that scholastic philosophy was to develop. The scope of the **quadrivium** was very limited. It began with simple Arithmetic, including the use of the abacus or counting board – very necessary for calculations with Roman numerals. Geometry was studied in Euclid. Astronomy dealt with the heavenly bodies and their movements as then understood. Finally came Music – the theory of the relation of the scale of notes to numbers and to the harmony of the universe.

Since, however, the schools existed for the purpose of training the clergy all these secular subjects were subservient to and intended merely as a preparation for theology, which was not yet, as it later became, a formal and systematic science. It consisted in a deep and prolonged study of Scripture and of its interpretation as found in the commentaries of the great Latin Fathers, especially Saint Augustine. These commentaries dealt not only with the literal meaning of the books but also with their allegorical and figurative senses as vehicles of Christian doctrine and moral teaching.

«The ordinary method of instruction was for the teacher in any subject to start with a reading of the text of the prescribed authority, which owing to the scarcity of books, had often to be committed to memory by the students. He would then expound the text and dictate his commentary upon it...... Differences of interpretation gave rise to various problems, which were posed and answered by the teacher with the aid of the views of the authorities.» (a)

(a) «A History of Europe from 911 to 1198» by Z.N. Brooke, p. 385.

Such in outline would have been Norbert's education; we know that he had the best then available and that he took full advantage of it. However the bent of his mind was more practical than academic and it was not as an intellectual that he was to make his mark in the world. So in early manhood he went to the court of the Archbishop of Cologne, Frederick of Carinthia, where he could receive the necessary training to fit him for high office in the Church. The archbishops of Cologne at this period in addition to their pre-eminence in the Church ranked among the leading princes of Germany. Norbert remained for several years at the archbishop's court where he was very successful and popular. It must have been about this time, although we have no record of the date, that he was ordained subdeacon.

Some time after 1106 he moved on to the court of King Henry V, being appointed as one of the clerks of the Chapel Royal, whose main functions were to celebrate the Divine Office and to carry out the work of the Royal Chancery, which gave them a thorough training in drawing up charters and other official documents as well as an opportunity to become familiar with the affairs of state and the work of government. It was from their ranks that bishops were commonly chosen and it must have seemed that advancement could not be slow in coming to one so richly gifted and well connected as Norbert.

His earliest biographer gives us a description of how he appeared to his contemporaries at this period. Handsome, slim and athletic in build, he was slightly above the average height. Wealthy and aristocratic, he had every advantage that the world could offer and was successful in everything that he undertook. A born leader and a man of great natural charm, he won the esteem and liking of all who came to know him. He was of a cheerful and equable temperament, friendly and a good mixer, and got on easily with men of every class – rich and poor, learned and simple. He was generous and found greater pleasure in giving than in receiving.

He was a man of fastidious tastes for whom nothing but the best was ever good enough, whether it was thoroughbred horses or fine clothes and rich furnishings more suitable for a courtier than for a churchman. Unfortunately his parents seem to have spoiled him, being too easygoing and never denying him anything. So now he threw himself wholeheartedly into the life of the court and gave himself up to pleasure and self-indulgence, although there is no reason to think his conduct was ever actually immoral and certainly no breath of scandal ever touched him. He lived only for the present moment, wasting all his splendid natural gifts. Religion played little part in his life at this time and he never paused to think where all of this was leading him. Worldly success, popularity at court, the admiration and applause of others, all encouraged him in this way of life and held out the promise of a successful career as the world reckons success.

Once Henry was firmly established on the throne it became apparent that his attitude to the Church differed in no way from that of his father and he vehemently asserted his claim to appoint bishops and invest them with ring and crozier, the insignia of their spiritual office. This brought him into conflict with the Pope, who now reaffirmed the decrees against lay investiture and severely censured all who disregarded them. Henry, anxious to be crowned as Emperor, decided for the moment to adopt a more conciliatory approach and sent an embassy to the Pope, who agreed to crown him but refused to compromise on investiture. So in the summer of 1110, in accordance with custom, the King summoned a large army to accompany him from Germany to Rome and Norbert went with it as one of the royal chaplains.

The Pope at this time was Paschal II (1099-1118), a Tuscan by birth. He was a monk, like the last three Popes, and had been abbot of Saint Lawrence-without-the-Walls when Gregory VII made him a cardinal. Devout and strict in his personal life, he was a good monk and an excellent subordinate who could be relied on to carry out instructions to the letter but he was quite unfitted by character and temperament to rule. Lacking in understanding of the world and its ways, he was rigid in his interpretation of the laws and uncompromising in their application but weak when faced with determined opposition.

In his simplicity he made a truly astounding proposal when he heard that the King was approaching Rome. The clergy would renounce all their temporalities, including all the offices, jurisdictions and lands that they held from the King, who would in return give up the ceremony of investiture. This would have wrecked the whole frame-work of society but the King readily accepted the proposal, knowing that it could never be carried out, and left the impossible task of enforcing it to the unworldly Paschal.

On the appointed day the King entered Rome and was given a great welcome by the people, who led him in procession to Saint Peter's where the Pope was waiting for him. When the agreement to renounce temporalities was announced it was very badly received and there were angry protests. However the ceremony began and the King knelt before the Pope in the customary act of reverence but when the latter raised him up to give him the kiss of peace, he suddenly showed his real intentions, calling out in German to his soldiers who promptly surrounded the Pope and the cardinals and took Paschal as a prisoner to their camp outside the city.

Norbert, who had been in close attendance on the King was deeply shocked by this act of treachery and sacrilege in which he felt himself to have been implicated, albeit involuntarily. So he made his way into the presence of the Pope and, falling to his knees, expressed his sorrow and asked for pardon, which the Pope willingly gave him.

Meanwhile the soldiers had killed a number of the Romans whom they had taken by surprise, and were plundering the countryside. In this way and by threats the King wore down the resistance of his captive, who gave in completely at the end of two months and surrendered to him the appointment and investiture of bishops. The imperial coronation now took place and the newly crowned Emperor returned to Germany. As was to be expected the Pope's craven capitulation provoked vigorous complaints from bishops and abbots everywhere and bitter accusations that he had betrayed the Church. The pressure on him was so strong that in March 1112 at a Council held in the Lateran he completely revoked the grant that he had made and expressed his regret for his weakness but he refused to excommunicate the Emperor.

Meanwhile in Germany, where unity had been weakened by the troubles of Henry IV's long reign, the Emperor, who was engaged in a constant struggle to assert his authority against the nobles, now had the bishops against him too. Norbert was still at court and high in the Emperor's favour so that when the rich and important diocese of Cambrai fell vacant in June 1113, the Emperor pressed it on him and was reluctant to accept his refusal as final. We are not told what Norbert's reasons were but doubtless his loyalty to the Church would not allow him to accept investiture by a layman, particularly in the light to recent events, whilst however worldly he might be, he always had a certain integrity of spirit which would not allow him to become a priest without being ready to live up to the obligations of the priesthood.

CHAPTER II

CONVERSION.

One day in the spring or early summer of the year 1115 Norbert, who had left the court and was living at Xanten, set out, wearing his finest clothes, to ride to Vreden some 15 miles away, accompanied only by a single page. It was a beautiful day when they started and the country was looking its best, but after they had gone some distance the sky became overcast and threatening and soon they found themselves at the centre of an appalling thunderstorm. The terrified page begged Norbert to turn back but, although he was frightened, he insisted on pressing ahead and, in any case, they were far from shelter. Suddenly there was a terrific crash and a blinding flash as the lightning struck the ground immediately in front of Norbert, who was thrown senseless from his horse. The shock brought him to a knowledge of himself and, when at length he returned to consciousness, he experienced a deep sense of the presence of God and a bitter regret for his past sins. He turned to God in prayer : «Lord, what would you have me do ?» and the answer came to him in the depth of his soul in the words of the psalm : «Cease from evil and do good». From that moment Norbert was never to look back nor were there ever to be any compromises or half measures in his service of God, although it would be some time before he was to know to what work God was calling him. He returned at once to Xanten and never went back to the court of the Emperor nor to that of the Archbishop. His conversion was sudden and complete – a miracle of grace – but he did not make any immediate change in his outward style of life, although he began to wear a hairshirt under his rich clothes. It would be false, however, to imagine that his path was easy or that he was free from temptations and difficulties.

He felt the need now of a period of prayer and recollection, in order to learn God's will in his regard and to prepare himself to do it by deepening his spiritual life under the guidance of a wise and experienced director. So he went to the Benedictine abbey of Siegburg, which still stands today on a steep hill about twenty miles South of Cologne. It had been founded some fifty years earlier by Saint Anno, Archbishop of Cologne, and now under its third abbot, Conon, a saintly and learned man who was later to become Bishop of Regensburg, it was an important centre of religious life in Germany. His stay here had a profound and lasting influence on Norbert and served him as a kind of novitiate. In Conon he found complete understanding and a close friendship soon grew up between them. Here in the monastery he spent a considerable part of each day assisting at the Divine Office in the abbey church; the rest of his time, apart from his conferences with the abbot, he passed in private prayer and meditation, and in the study of the Scriptures of which he learned some parts by heart since bibles were then too scarce to become personal possessions. It soon became clear to him that, great as were his admiration and affection for the monks, he was not called to an enclosed contemplative life but rather to combine the priestly apostolate with the religious life. How this was to be done he did not know yet but God would make it plain in His own time.

In those days ordinations were customarily held during

24

the Advent Ember Days, which in 1115 were from 15 to 18 December, and shortly before that Norbert came to the Archbishop of Cologne and asked to be accepted as a candidate for Orders. The Archbishop expressed great surprise, because Norbert had so often refused ordination when it had been offered to him in the past, but said how happy he was to grant his wish now. When, however, he went on to ask that he might receive the diaconate and the priesthood on the same day, which could not be done without a special dispensation, the Archbishop was quite taken aback and demanded the reason for this sudden and unexpected request. At first Norbert was reluctant to speak about himself but, when the archbishop continued to press him, he realized that in the circumstances he had a right to know the secrets of his conscience. Accordingly he told him all that had happened since his experience on the road to Vreden. He ended by kneeling with tears in his eyes to make a full confession of all his past sins and to promise a thorough amendment of his life. The Archbishop, deeply impressed by his sincerity, decided after a long and careful consideration that, although it was against all precedent, it would be in the interests of the Church that he should grant the dispensation.

When the long awaited day came the cathedral was crowded and many of those who knew Norbert, even if only by reputation, came out of curiosity. He arrived dressed in his richest and most splendid apparel and joined the other ordinands, who were already vested. When the sacristan came to give him his vestments he made a sign to one of his servants, who was standing close by holding a coarse tunic of lambskin such as hermits and pilgrims wore, and taking off his rich fur-lined mantle he clothed himself in it to the astonishment of the bystanders.

This may seem a somewhat theatrical gesture to us today, but it was one that his contemporaries understood, and in truth there was nothing theatrical about it. Much as Saint Francis was to do a century later, he wanted to humble his pride by making himself appear contemptible in the eyes of the frivolous and worldly companions who had hitherto admired him so greatly for the wrong reasons.

Immediately after his ordination he returned to Siegburg to prepare himself for his priestly ministry by a retreat of forty days and after that went back to Xanten to take up his duties as a canon. On the day following his arrival, in accordance with custom, as a newly ordained priest he celebrated the High Mass at the invitation of the Dean and Chapter. All went normally until after the gospel, when Norbert turned towards the congregation and began to preach. This first sermon of his evidently made a deep impression on those who heard it for it was still remembered years afterwards and recorded by his earliest biographer. He was to become one of the greatest preachers of his day and now he was speaking from his heart, following the inspiration of the moment and sharing with his hearers the fruits of his contemplation during the recent momentous months. He spoke of man's eternal destiny and of his life in this world, of the deceitfulness of its riches and pleasures, of its cares and perils and of the emptiness of worldly ambition. He warned them of the justice of God, that those who lead evil lives cannot escape punishment, quoting Saint Paul : «I warn you that those who do such things shall not inherit the kingdom of God». (Gal. 5. 21) In this sermon, although he did not name them nor address them directly, it was his fellow canons that he particularly had in mind. He knew that many of them were leading worldly, self-indulgent lives, just as he himself had done until recently, and he wanted to stir up their consciences and bring them to a realization of their spiritual danger.

On the next day he returned to the charge at the daily meeting of the Chapter when, addressing the Dean, he quoted the Rule of the Council of Aachen to which as secular canons they were bound and pleaded for its observance. The Dean and the seniors were inclined to listen to him but the younger canons, who had no wish to give up their pleasant way of life, grumbled amongst themselves and criticised him. He took the matter up again the following day in chapter, giving details of the breaches of the Rule that he had observed and naming the offenders. This chapter of faults may seem strange and disagreeable to us but it was the universal practice in religious communities in those days.

At first his colleagues, irritated though they might be, maintained an outward show of respect for Norbert but when he persisted day after day in his efforts to reform them, they found it intolerable and soon they formed a plan to silence him once and for all. They suborned a certain disreputable clerk in minor orders to act as their agent and this man, approaching Norbert publicly, began to insult him, using the vilest language, and finally spat full in his face. Norbert did not say a word but wiped his face and went away by himself to find comfort in prayer. He felt no resentment, recognizing that he had deserved this humiliation by his sins.

He saw clearly now that in the interests of peace he must leave Xanten, at least for a time. He had perhaps, in his zeal for reform, been too outspoken and lacking in tact but at all events the situation in the Chapter was now impossible.

At this period he became a frequent visitor at the Abbey of Siegburg as well as at an abbey of canons regular at Kloster-Rath, situated just north of Aachen, which had been founded some twelve years earlier and followed a very austere rule. It was here that an event occurred that made a deep impression on his contemporaries. One day, when he was saying mass in the crypt of the abbey church, just after consecration a large spider dropped into the chalice. At that time it was believed that a spider's bite was poisonous and could prove fatal. Norbert's reaction was a natural feeling of fear and repulsion which he quickly overcame and to avoid any chance of irreverence, however slight, he chose to risk his life by consuming the contents of the chalice including the spider. After Mass as he knelt in prayer, offering his life to God, he suddenly sneezed and out came the spider.

Most often, however, he would visit a hermit priest called Ludolph, who lived a life of great austerity and exercised his ministry not far from Xanten. He was a most saintly man, a lover of poverty and a fearless witness to the truth. His great reputation for holiness, however, did not save either him or his followers from countless threats and even actual violence from those of the clergy whom he rebuked for their evil lives.

It was at this period also that Norbert made a thorough study of the customs and manner of life of the different kinds of religious – canons regular, monks and hermits – hoping to learn from their example and base his own way of life on it.

After some months he returned to Xanten but did not go into residence with the Chapter again. In the suburbs there was a hill called Fürstenberg on which there stood a chapel on his family property and here he lived as a hermit for the next two years. He spent his time in prayer, reading and meditation and he said Mass every day, although at that time private masses were the exception rather than the rule. He also mortified himself by rigorous fasting and vigils; he often passed the whole night without sleep. He said that the practice of vigils was very fruitful, although trying physically.

His love of God always found expression in the love of his neighbour; contemplation overflowed into action. Like his Divine Master, «when he saw the crowds, he had compassion for them, because they were harassed and helpless, like sheep without a shepherd». (Mt. 9, 36) So he would leave his solitude from time to time to go out to preach to the people.

Soon the hostility towards him spread among the clergy far beyond the circle of his colleagues at Xanten. His example was a reproach to those who were leading unworthy lives whilst many felt resentment that a newly ordained priest and one so recently converted should, as they saw it, presume to take so much upon himself; they cast doubt on his sincerity and severely criticised his whole manner of living. One such critic was Rupert of Deutz, a monk who later became abbot of a monastery near Cologne. He must have made Norbert's acquaintance when they were both staying at Siegburg where he lent him a book that he had written. He complained that Norbert having kept it for several months, returned it without comment and had then gone about telling others that it contained false doctrine. It appeared that the passage in question was somewhat ambiguous and that Norbert had misunderstood it. When this was explained to him, as Rupert himself allowed, he readily admitted his mistake and made a handsome apology. Rupert was a man who took offence easily and made a number of enemies, some of whom adversely criticised his works. Norbert had no doubt been carried away by his zeal and been too hasty but certainly he was not inspired by malice or jealousy as Rupert claimed.

The opposition continued to grow and eventually came to a head at the Council of Fritzlar which had been summoned by the papal legate, Conon, Cardinal Bishop of Praeneste, to condemn the Emperor and the anti-pope whom he had just set up. It assembled on 26th July, 1118, and to it came archbishops, bishops and abbots from the whole of Germany together with a large gathering of clergy and laity. Norbert's enemies took advantage of the occasion to denounce him and he was summoned to appear before the council. Two main accusations were brought against him : – first that he had taken upon himself the office of preaching without authority and, secondly, that he had worn a religious habit, although he did not belong to any religious order, and had made himself singular by wearing sheepskins or goatskins instead of the dress appropriate for a secular canon, especially one who was a nobleman.

These accusations were made out of malice and Norbert's reply was brief and to the point : –

As regards preaching; a priest is empowered to preach at his ordination when the bishop says : «Receive the power to proclaim the word of God».

As for the religious life : Scripture says : «Religion pure and undefiled is this : to visit orphans and widows in their affliction and to keep oneself unstained from the world».

As for clothing : Saint Peter teaches that it is not in our outward adornment that God takes pleasure.

The council did not condemn him nor did it clear him. The reason why it arrived at no conclusion is not known, whether it was lack of time or because the case raised embarrassing questions for some of those present.

Norbert left the council in a mood of dejection, feeling utterly isolated and friendless. He turned to God for help and spent the whole night in prayer, asking for guidance and strength. Finally towards dawn he was overcome by exhaustion and fell asleep with his chin resting on his hands. He woke with a start and in his weariness felt tempted to give up the struggle, since he had not succeeded even in keeping awake for a single night but he recognized the temptation as a suggestion of the Evil One and firmly rejected it.

CHAPTER III

THE MISSIONER.

Back at Xanten Norbert took stock of his position and, after much prayerful deliberation, finally came to a decision about his future. He had now been a priest for almost three years and was forced to recognize that he could no longer hope to do any good, by preaching or example, where he was. On the contrary his mere presence was a constant provocation to the malice of his enemies and thus a threat to peace and harmony. Hitherto he had considered that as a canon of Xanten it was his duty to serve the Church there; the outcome of the Council of Fritzlar was a clear sign to him that this was no longer the case and that he was now free to leave all things and follow Christ like the Apostles.

He went, therefore, to the Archbishop to ask his blessing and to resign his canonry at Xanten and all his other benefices. Then he sold all his property and gave the proceeds to the poor. His property on the Fürstenberg, where he had been living latterly, he gave to the Abbey of Siegburg for a dependant priory to be established there. He and his elder brother gave three farms to endow it and the latter also gave another property for the repose of the soul of a third brother who had been killed in battle. All Norbert kept, in addition to his vestments and a mass kit, was a pack mule and a small sum of money for travelling expenses. It is pleasant to note that he gave a precious chalice that he had used himself, as a parting gift to the canons of Xanten to show that he bore them no ill will.

It was late in September or in October 1118 that he left Xanten for good, accompanied by two laymen who had been in his service but were now to be his brothers in religion. A few days later they arrived at the little town of Huy, on the Meuse between Liège and Namur, where he gave away to the poor the mule and all his money, for he thought that he must keep nothing for himself if he would really follow Christ in His poverty. So now, taking only what he needed to say Mass, he went on his way with his companions, barefoot, wearing a woollen tunic and cloak, making no provision for their lodging and often sleeping out of doors.

His route lay southward through Burgundy and along the valley of the Rhone for he had made up his mind to submit his case to the judgement of the Pope. Paschal II had died in the previous January and had been succeeded by Cardinal John of Gaeta, who had done good work as papal chancellor under the last two popes and now took the name of Gelasius II. The new Pope was not long in Rome for on the news of his election the Emperor lost no time in going there to set up his anti-pope, Maurice Burdin, under the name of Gregory VIII. Gelasius took refuge with the Normans in South Italy and then, after, an unsuccessful attempt to return to Rome, went to France, where he set up his court at Saint-Gilles in Provence, near Nîmes. Norbert will have heard of this and so it was to Saint-Gilles that he made his way, arriving sometime in December.

Having obtained an audience with the Pope, he asked for and was granted absolution from his fault in receiving the diaconate and the priesthood on the same day for, in spite of the dispensation, this had been troubling his conscience. He told the Pope his whole history and confided to him his hopes and aspirations. Gelasius, greatly impressed by his evident ability and zeal in God's service, was anxious to keep him at the papal court but Norbert became alarmed at the suggestion and begged to be excused. He would not refuse to obey but he urged his inexperience as well as the penitential life to which he had bound himself in reparation for his years of self indulgence at the courts of the King and the Archbishop. Let the Pope put him under obedience to become a canon, monk or hermit, or even to live as a pilgrim, and he would gladly obey. Gelasius, recognizing the sincerity of the man before him, his strength of character and his deeply religious disposition, gave him permission and indeed officially commissioned him to preach anywhere in the world, confirming the grant by letters issued under his seal.

Having thus received his mission from the Pope, Norbert set out with his companions on the return journey. The winter was exceptionally severe and their progress was necessarily slow as they walked along the icy roads, sometimes sinking knee deep in the snow, or even deeper where it had drifted. He spared himself none of his accustomed austerities and vigils and during Lent observed the fast strictly, not eating until the evening, except on Sunday, and seldom taking fish or wine. At Orleans he was joined by a young subdeacon, who brought their number up to four.

They came to Valenciennes on 22 March, 1119, and on the next day, which was Palm Sunday, Norbert preached in one of the city churches although he knew very little French, never having learned the language. The congregation must have had the greatest difficulty in following him but somehow he got his message across to them and his sermon made a deep impression on all who heard it.

His strong but sympathetic personality, his obvious sincerity and sanctity must have had their effect but above all it was the work of the Holy Spirit.

Seeing how exhausted he was everyone tried to persuade him to stay for a while and rest but he declined, being anxious to press on quickly to Germany where he would know the language and could begin his missionary work. Nevertheless he was forced to remain, for his companions suddenly fell ill and he had to look after them. He bathed their ulcers, nursed them, went out to beg food for them, prepared and served their meals but, in spite of all his care they died in the following week, Easter Week, and were buried, the two laymen in Saint Peter's near the market place and the subdeacon, who had become a monk on his deathbed, in Notre Dame, the principal church in the town.

Meanwhile it happened that on Wednesday in Holy Week Burchard, Bishop of Cambrai, whom Norbert had known well at the imperial court arrived in Valenciennes and Norbert, hearing of it, went to call on him. Outside the house where the bishop was staying he met one of his chaplains and asked if he would obtain an interview for him. The chaplain went in and told the bishop of the man who was waiting outside, barefoot in the freezing weather, and was told to bring him in. Norbert addressed the bishop in German but it was not until they had been speaking for a little while that the latter recognized the strange caller as his old friend. He was shocked and yet deeply moved to see him so emaciated and so poorly clad in the bitter cold. He could no longer restrain himself and, bursting into tears, embraced him. «Norbert, Norbert», he said, «who could ever have imagined that you would come to this ?» The chaplain, who could not understand what they were saying, since they spoke in German, was amazed at what he saw and asked the bishop afterwards who his visitor had been. «That man whom you have just seen», was the reply, «lived with me in the royal household when we were at court together. He was a man of noble birth and great wealth and was offered the bishopric which I now hold but refused to accept it.» When he heard this the chaplain could no longer keep back his own tears, not only because he was affected by seeing his bishop weeping but because he had long cherished a secret ambition, which he had confided to no one, of leaving the world and living like this man. Accordingly he made discreet inquiries to discover what road Norbert would be taking, but the latter now fell seriously ill himself and the bishop delayed his departure so as to see that he was properly cared for. Every day he sent one of his household to visit him and very often it was the young chaplain who went and so became deeply attached to him. When at last Norbert was better he came to him and told him of his secret aspirations, promising to join him on his journeys and share his life, if he would have him. Norbert was overjoyed and thanked God for sending him a companion. He was, therefore, disappointed when the young man said that he must first go to set his affairs in order but he replied that if his vocation was from God nothing would destroy it. The young man promised to come back and said that nothing could ever break the bond between him and Norbert. This earliest of Norbert disciples was Hugh of Fosses and we shall hear a great deal more about him.

During his convalescence Norbert evidently worked hard at his French for it will be among the French-speaking inhabitants of what is today Southern Belgium that we shall next find him preaching. He visited Cambrai at the end of May, perhaps to see Burchard who was to prove a loyal friend over the years. It was in June that Hugh rejoined him, to his great joy, and they set out on their missionary work, visiting the towns and villages; preaching, settling quarrels and reconciling enemies.

It was to those who were the most neglected spiritually, the simple uneducated country people, that Norbert went by preference and it was not long before he won their admiration and love. His way of life, so unlike anything that they had ever known before, appealed to them for he and his companion took quite literally the words of Our Lord to the Apostles when he sent them out two by two : to take nothing for their journey, no bread, no money, no spare tunic. All that they took was what was needed for their work : a mass kit, a psalter and a few other books. They were soon, however, compelled to get a donkey for Norbert to ride when he was too tired to walk, for, unsparing of himself in his work, he yet relaxed nothing of his accustomed austerities.

He ate his meals seated on the ground, using his knees as a table; his only seasoning was salt and he drank nothing but water. The only exception was when he was invited to meals by bishops or abbots and consideration for others demanded that he should behave as they did and eat what he was offered. Neither he nor Hugh would accept anything for themselves and, if offerings were made at Mass which they could not refuse, they distributed them among the poor and the lepers. They trusted in the goodness of God to provide for all their needs, living in the world like pilgrims and strangers. Norbert thought that it would be disgraceful for anyone who had given up all for Christ to become enslaved by worthless trifles or petty gains. Affable and pleasant to everyone, although he could be stern when the occasion demanded, he showed special kindness to simple, ordinary folk and it is not surprising that they took him to their hearts. He had such a love for them that he would often forgo the hospitality of monasteries and castles so that he might lodge among them and be able to welcome any who wished to see him. His preaching was simple, direct and forceful and was supported by the example of his own life. Moreover his conversion had in no way diminished his natural charm or attractive personality so that time spent in his company or listening to him seemed all too short.

When he and his companion approached a town or village the shepherds would leave their flocks and hurry to spread the news of their arrival. The bells would be rung and everyone, men and women, old and young from every walk of life would hasten to the church to assist at Norbert's Mass and to hear him preach. After Mass and the sermon he would meet the people and talk with them, answering all their questions. These talks were of a practical nature, with a bearing on their everyday lives, on such subjects as regular confession, the practice of self denial, the married life, the right use of property and how to live a truly christian life in the world. Towards evening, when all their questions had been answered, the people would take the missioners to the house where they were to stay for the night and there was keen competition for the privilege of being Norbert's host.

Soon, as his reputation grew, he was invited to preach to the clergy or in monasteries. On these occasions his sermon would be followed by a conference at which many searching questions would be asked on such topics as the priesthood, the monastic life, the mutual relations and duties of superiors and their subjects, the problem of undeserved suffering, how men will be judged, the last end of man and the happiness of heaven. Most of the questions were prompted by an honest desire for knowledge but some were intended to test his sincerity or even to set traps for him so as to discredit his preaching, but he saw through their wiles and brought them to nothing by the unaffected simplicity of his replies.

In spite of all the other demands made on him he did not neglect the spiritual formation of his companion, whose coming had brought him so much joy. He realized that the extreme austerity and poverty of their life might frighten or dishearten him and so he set out to encourage and strengthen him. His aim was to lead him gently away from worldly desires that can never satisfy the heart of man, to bring him to Christ as the source of all life and to show him how to seek and find God. He spoke of the difficulties to be overcome and the virtues to be cultivated. Day by day he made it his special care to train Hugh for God's work.

Unfortunately very little has come down to us in detail about this part of Norbert's life, although one of his early biographers tells us that there was a great deal more that could usefully have been written. The incidents that are recorded cover only a few days but they give a vivid picture of Norbert as a peacemaker in an age of unbridled violence when men only too often took the law into their own hands and blood feuds were rife, whilst private wars were a common occurence.

One day, when he was passing through Fosses, a small walled town near Namur that was the home of Hugh, he found a number of people, clerics and layfolk, who had gathered to see him because they were interested by all that they had heard about him and particularly because they knew his companion personally. Being aware of his reputation as an apostle of peace, they pressed him to stay a little while with them, telling him of a deadly feud that had broken out in the neighbourhood in which some sixty people had lost their lives and which all the efforts of the religious and civil authorities had failed to end. As they were speaking a young man came that way whose brother had been murdered that very week because of the feud. When the bystanders caught sight of him they said : «Look ! here comes one of the men about whom we have been talking». Whereupon Norbert called to the man and gave him a friendly greeting. «My friend», he said, «I am a stranger and I have not asked a favour of anyone since I came here. It would give me great pleasure if you were the first to do me a kindness. Please do not refuse me». Norbert's words touched the heart of the young man and he replied : «Father, how could anyone refuse you». When he was asked to forgive his brother's murderer, not only did he agree at once but offered his help in bringing the feud to an end.

On the following Saturday both sides gathered at the near-by village of Moustier and a great many people came from the surrounding country, partly to see Norbert and partly to urge the enemies to make peace. Norbert remained praying in his room until nine o'clock and the crowd, tired of waiting began to grumble. In the end they demanded that Hugh, should go in and tell Norbert that unless he came out at once they would all go away. Hugh was nervous about doing so because he did not like to disturb Norbert at his prayers but at last they became so insistent that he summoned up the courage to go in. He spoke diffidently to Norbert telling him what the people were saying and in a little while the latter came out.

First he said the Saturday Mass of Our Lady followed by a requiem Mass for all who had lost their lives in the feud. Then he began to preach; there were very few still present, since most had gone away as it was long past their normal meal time. As soon as he began to speak people left their food and drink on the table and hurried to hear him. When Norbert saw that the church was full he brought his sermon to an end and addressed the people like this : –

«Brethren, Our Lord Jesus Christ, when he sent out His disciples to preach, told them that into whatever house they entered they should first say : 'Peace to this house'. We follow their example and offer you that same peace, the true and lasting peace. You must not close your minds and reject it. You all know why we have come here today but we can achieve nothing by ourselves. It is only God who is able to help you; your part is to accept his Will wholeheartedly». When he had finished speaking they all said that they were willing to do whatever he told them in God's Name. So without any further ado both parties went out in front of the church, renounced their quarrel and swore a solemn oath to live in peace for the future.

The next morning he rose very early and went to the village of Gembloux, a short distance away, where he was welcomed enthusiastically not merely on account of his reputation as a preacher but because it was hoped that he might give the people the peace that they longed for. The whole district had been ravaged and reduced almost to a desert by two lords who were waging a relentless war against each other, pillaging and burning everywhere. When they told him about this, Norbert, moved by their appeal and grieved by the sufferings of the poor country people, went at once to find the two lords. He came to the first and spoke to him thus : «You are an important and powerful man but you must not forget that it is from God that your power comes. I come to you in His Name to ask you to forgive this man who has wronged you. If you do that you will bring comfort to the poor and unfortunate and win pardon for your own sins». The lord examined his visitor closely and was impressed because he was so poorly dressed and unassuming and yet spoke so persuasively. His heart was touched and he replied : «Be it as you wish, for it would be against all reason to refuse this request of yours». Then he went to see the other lord but here he was met by an obdurate refusal even to listen. The man burst into a stream of violent abuse so that it was quite plain that any further attempt to speak to him would be worse than useless. Norbert remarked to his companion : «The man is mad. Very soon he will fall into the hands of his enemies who will ill-treat him». So saying he turned and left but within a week what he had foretold came to pass for this lord was captured by his enemies and thrown into prison.

Going on to the next village, Couroy, he found that people had come in from all the surrounding district to hear him. After he had finished Mass and made his customary appeal for peace and reconciliation, he asked his hearers whether there were any disputes amongst them and by his tact brought about a peaceful settlement of some long-standing quarrels. There was one man, however, a knight, whom all his efforts at persuassion could not influence. In the end he rushed out angrily and leapt on to his horse to ride away but, although he kept on spurring it furiously, the animal would not move. In the meantime the congregation came out of the church and others came running up from all sides to see what was causing the commotion. They looked on in astonishment; some were in tears but others began to laugh at him. Full of embarassment, the knight went back into the church and, kneeling down to ask for pardon, now willingly accepted the proposals for peace that he had rejected before.

CHAPTER IV

PRÉMONTRÉ.

Shortly after Norbert left him Pope Gelasius had gone to the great abbey of Cluny, intending to carry out a visitation of various churches, but had fallen ill and had died on 29th January, 1119. The cardinals who had accompanied him proceeded without delay to elect his successor at Cluny, since Rome was still in the hands of the anti-pope. On 2 February they chose Guy, archbishop of Vienne, who took the name of Calixtus II. He was an able statesman, a lover of peace but not to be intimidated by threats or force, and it was he who had taken the lead in bringing Paschal II to revoke the concessions on invest-iture that had been wrung from him by the Emperor. He was also extremely well connected, being related to the Emperor and being paternal uncle to the Queen of France. He summoned a council to meet at Rheims on 20 October to confirm his election and to carry out various reforms. It was attended by some four hundred and twenty six archbishops, bishops and abbots, who came from all parts of Western Europe with their numerous retinues, and the King of France himself, Louis VI, was also present.

Norbert, who seems to have been recently in the neigh-bourhood of Cologne, (3) went to Rheims with Hugh and

(3) The charter issued about this date (August or September 1119) to confirm the foundation on the Fürstenberg is given «coram testibus Norberto et fratre ejus Heriberto (in the presence of Norbert and his brother Heribert as witnesses)».

another cleric who had joined them lately, hoping to obtain an audience with the new Pope so that he might ask for a renewal of his authority to preach and for approval of his way of life. When he arrived, he found that none of the great prelates or their busy chaplains had time to spare for anyone so insignificant as this gaunt, barefoot ascetic in his rough tunic. Certainly it was not to be expected that the Holy Father should put aside his responsibilities, even for a moment, to attend to the private affairs of such a person and so, finding the papal antechambers always crowded with princes and prelates, Norbert saw that he had no hope of getting an audience. After three days, having achieved nothing, he left Rheims, utterly disheartened, not knowing where to go next. He had gone about five miles out of the city when he had a strange experience; suddenly he heard two voices, one of which said : «Here comes Norbert with his two companions», to which the other replied : «No ! Here comes Norbert with his one companion». There was nobody in sight anywhere and the voices seemed to come from above. Completely baffled he turned aside to investigate, but could find no explanation and so, full of amazement, he sat down by the roadside with his companions and looked around. They had not been there long when a bishop, with his retinue of clergy and lay attendants, came riding towards them on his way to Rheims. When he saw them sitting there the bishop stopped to speak to them, greeting them kindly and asked who they were. Norbert replied that he came from Lorraine, that he had left his home and given up the world to adopt the religious life. He told how he had gone to Rheims to seek counsel and obtain the authority of the Holy See for his way of life; how he had been there three days but had found it impossible to see the Pope on account of the continual stream of important people going in and out; how he left the city sad and despondent and did not know where to turn. The bishop was touched by what he heard and invited them to go back to Rheims with him, promising to introduce them to the Pope. Seeing that they were on foot, he told some of his retainers to dismount and let them have their horses so that they could ride with him and he might get to know them better. On the way Hugh told him all about Norbert : how he came of a noble family and had been rich but had given it all up for a life of voluntary poverty.

The working of Providence can be clearly discerned in this meeting which was to have a decisive effect on Norbert's life and work. The bishop was Bartholomew de Joux, Bishop of Laon, a nephew of the Pope and a cousin, through his mother, of the King of France. He was about the same age as Norbert and, having been brought up by his uncle, Manasses, Archbishop of Rheims, had been appointed as a young subdeacon to a canonry in the metropolitan chapter. Gentle and unassuming though he was, he proved himself to be a natural leader and a capable administrator. Yet he never lost the simplicity of soul and deep religious sense that gave him a sympathetic understanding of the ascetic and contemplative tendencies which found their outlet in the new monastic orders. (He was, indeed, at the end of his life to resign his bishopric and end his days as a simple Cistercian monk). When he was unanimously elected Bishop of Laon in 1113 he accepted, knowing well that he was taking on a heritage that none would envy him. The previous Easter there had been a rising of the populace against the unworthy Bishop Gaudry in which he was killed. In the rioting that ensued many lost their lives, whilst the cathedral, the bishop's palace, the canons' close, ten churches and a large number of private houses had been burned down.

Bartholomew set himself to rebuild the cathedral without delay and was so successful, having collected money in England and France, that it was ready to be consecrated in two years. The moral and spiritual state of the diocese was equally deplorable and this too the new bishop took in hand energetically as well as becoming a great patron of learning in the cathedral school of Laon, which flourished under the two famous brothers, Anselm and Ralph.

On his arrival in Rheims the bishop was received by the Pope and took the opportunity to suggest respectfully that it was not good that the common father of all should only speak with the rich while the poor were kept away from him. The Pope readily agreed and the bishop was able to present Norbert and his companions who were graciously received. At Norbert's request he was given letters renewing his authority to preach everywhere but, owing to the heavy pressure of business, the Pope could not talk with them as much as he would have wished nor give adequate consideration to their future. Accordingly he promised to go to Laon as soon as the council was finished and to remain there a few days when everything could be discussed at leisure. He asked that they should be sent on ahead to await his arrival. He was evidently particularly concerned about the state of Norbert's health for he placed him in the personal care of the Bishop.

Now that he had been so well received by the Pope the bishops and abbots all made him welcome, going to hear him preach and consulting him on various matters. Most of all they were impressed by the extreme austerity of his life, which many of them tried to persuade him to mitigate somewhat for the sake of his health, but without success. During the rest of his time in Rheims the Bishop kept

Norbert and his companions with him and insisted that they stay with him on his return home.

At Laon Norbert found some of his relations on his mother's side living in the district and he spent some time with them during the next few months. They were shocked when they saw how emaciated and utterly worn out he was and begged the Bishop to take charge of him and look after him until he was better, whether he liked it or not. They need not have troubled to do so for the Bishop had already made up his mind to do all that he could to keep him in his diocese. A deep and lasting friendship had grown up between them and more than twenty years later, recalling the events of this winter in a charter issued in 1143, Bartholomew was to write of his great admiration and love for his friend – «Norbert, a man distinguished by his piety, whom we came to know well and to value for his holiness, integrity, learning and eloquence. After many times entreating him we prevailed on him to pass the winter (of 1119-1120) with us. The more we listened to him and the closer our friendship with him became, the more we found pleasure and refreshment of spirit in his company. When the winter was almost over and that holy man wished to leave us, we were petitioned by the dignitaries of our church and by many members of the nobility to establish him somewhere in our diocese where he might serve God, a thing close to our own heart. It was only with the greatest difficulty that we succeeded at last, by the help of God's grace in winning his consent.»

Norbert was more ready than he might otherwise have been to spend the winter at Laon since he had just lost his fellow worker, Hugh. As long as they had been in his own country, around Fosses, the latter had remained with him, although without changing his secular dress for a religious habit. When they left Rheims he had gone back to Cambrai with Bishop Burchard, explaining that he still had certain affairs to settle and obligations to discharge. Eighteen months were to pass before his return. It is true that Norbert still had one companion but, since he was not a priest, he could not replace Hugh in their missionary partnership.

At this time the cathedral school of Laon had a great reputation and scholars came to it from Italy, Spain, Germany, England and even further afield. Norbert decided to take the opportunity of following a course of lectures on Psalm 118, «They are happy whose life is blameless», a long psalm on the excellence of God's law and the happiness of those who live by it, a portion of which is recited on most days in the Divine Office. When this came to the ears of Drogo, a monk who had been at one time a fellow student with Norbert, he wrote to him, sternly taking him to task for deserting the divine wisdom in favour of human learning. Norbert accepted the rebuke and ceased to attend the lectures; in any case he knew that his vocation was not to a life of learning but to missionary work amongst ordinary folk. Drogo was to have a distinguished career, becoming eventually Cardinal Bishop of Ostia.

It was at this time that a devout lady called Helvide, who had heard of his reputation for sanctity, came from Soissons to ask Norbert's advice. She confided to him her sorrow that she had no children though she had been married for several years. She and her husband, she said, had married in the hope of having children and she would rather separate from him and leave the world than live together childless. «No», replied Norbert, «You will soon have a son. You will not bring him up for a worldly career but will consecrate him to God from the moment of his birth. You will have others after him and, in the end you

and they will give yourselves to God in the religious life.»
She believed him and was not disappointed for a son was
born whom she christened Nicholas. He died while still
a deacon but lived to see his father and mother and all
their other children enter the religious life.

As he had promised, the Pope came to Laon as soon
as he could and was received with great honour by the
Bishop. They both gave careful consideration to Norbert's
future and the Pope had several long talks with him,
which only served to confirm the favourable impression
that he had already formed of his character, ideals and
way of life. He and the Bishop were convinced that here
was a man who could render immense service to the
Church but they saw that, if his work was to have its full
effect and achieve permanent results, he must cease to
be a freelance and must work within the framework of
an established religious society. A suitable opportunity
seemed to offer itself in a community of canons regular
that the bishop had founded beside the small church of
Saint Martin, just outside the walls of Laon. The foundation had not proved successful and the Bishop was now
left with it on his hands. So he suggested to the Pope that
Norbert should be appointed as superior, and he tried to
persuade him to accept the office. Norbert replied that it
was not to seek a benefice at Laon that he had given up
his rich preferments at Cologne and in any case he did
not wish to settle in a city but in a solitary and desert
place. The Pope, however, supported the bishop who
now got the canons to elect Norbert. At first he tried
hard to decline but, when the Pope insisted on his acceptance, he agreed for fear of causing offence or incurring
the guilt of disobedience. He felt obliged, though, in all
humility to make his position quite clear. «Holy Father»,
He said, «I am sure that you will remember that the work

of preaching has twice been assigned to me as my duty, first by your predecessor of happy memory and later by yourself. However, lest I should seem to be seeking to have my own way, I accept, with due regard nevertheless to the way of life that I have undertaken, and which I cannot abandon without grave peril to my soul. I have promised to live like the Apostles, following the Gospel counsels of perfection. I do not refuse the task provided that the canons accept this way of life».

At first the canons of Saint Martin's were delighted to have as their superior a priest with such a great reputation and one, moreover, so high in the favour of the Pope and their own Bishop. But when it was explained to them what was meant by living according to the Gospel; how they must follow Christ, despising the world and practising voluntary poverty; how they must obey the precepts of their Rule, they quickly changed their minds. The ascetic appearance and uncompromising teaching of their new superior filled them with dismay. «We refuse to have this man over us,» they said, «Never have we or our predecessors known a master like him. We shall be deprived of our property and have no redress. No one will listen to our complaints. Let us be free to live as we have been accustomed. God's will is to correct and not to kill». It has been remarked that it is much easier to found a new monastery than to reform one that has become relaxed. In this case Norbert, who had only undertaken the task out of obedience and against his better judgement, was now free to leave with a good conscience.

He returned to the Bishop who made it his personal concern to see him fully restored to health and in return found much help and enjoyment in the conversation of his guest. He could not bear the thought of losing Norbert and used every possible argument to persuade him to remain in the diocese. He reminded him that he had said that he would settle in a «solitary and desert place». «There are many such places suitable for a monastery in the diocese,» he said, «which I shall show you and I shall give you whichever you choose». He had the support of many of the leading men, both among the clergy and the laity, in his efforts to win over Norbert. When at last he did agree the bishop went out with him each day to show him some church that might suit him or some place where a community could settle and build a monastery.

First he took him to Foigny, some twenty five miles North of Laon, in the great forest of Thierarche, where he showed him an ideal site for a monastery with arable land, pastures, wood and water. After reflection and prayer Norbert gave his answer : «Indeed this place is entirely suitable for a monastery but God does not intend it for me». (So it proved when in the following year, at the request of Bishop Bartholomew, Saint Bernard sent a colony of Cistercian monks who made a foundation that soon grew into a flourishing abbey.) On their way back to Laon they visited another place in the forest, called Thenailles. Again Norbert prayed for light and again he answered that it was a good site for a monastery but not meant for him. Ten years later the bishop was to remember this visit when he established a monastery of White Canons there.

Next the bishop took Norbert into the rugged, heavily wooded district known today as the massif of Saint-Gobain, which then formed part of the vast forest of Voas. Following a little used road they came, about eleven miles South West of Laon, to a narrow valley whose steep sides were covered by the tall forest trees. Here there stood a chapel dedicated to Saint John the Baptist which had fallen into disrepair. It belonged to the Abbey of Saint Vincent of Laon but the monks had made no attempt to set up a house there since the site seemed quite unfit for human habitation, a wilderness of forbidding aspect, marshy, overgrown and impenetrable, with nothing to commend it except the chapel and, close at hand, an orchard and a small pond which was fed by water seeping in from the marsh and by the torrents that rushed down the mountain side when it rained. The chapel was served occasionally by a monk who came from the abbey to say Mass and left immediately afterwards, since few people came that way and there was nowhere that a meal could be obtained. The name of this unpromising place was Prémontré, a name that was soon to become famous throughout Christendom.

The Bishop went into the chapel with Norbert to pray and, when they had finished, suggested that they had better leave as it would soon be dark and there was nowhere in the vicinity where they could put up for the night. However Norbert asked to be allowed to remain by himself and pass the night in prayer. The bishop agreed and, as it was already becoming dusk, he rode as fast as he could with his attendants to his country house at Anizy, two or three miles away. He did not neglect Norbert, though, and sent him bread and whatever else he might need. Early next morning he went back to find out how he had fared and whether he had come to any decision. He found him exuberantly happy : «My lord and father,» he said, «here I shall remain for I know that this is the place chosen for me by God and here, through the grace of God, many will find salvation. Yet this chapel is not where they will have their mother house; it is on the other side of this hill that they will build their monastery. Last night I had a vision of a vast number of men in white habits carrying silver crosses, torches and thuribles, and singing as they went in procession». The bishop was delighted but, since he was anxious that the interests of the Abbey of Saint Martin should not suffer in any way, he asked the Abbot to come to see him and gave him a more valuable property in exchange. Then he gave the place to Norbert to be held freehold in perpetuity.

Much has been written about the name, Prémontré, some of it quite fanciful, but there seems to be no doubt that this is what the valley was already called, probably because a clearing had been made in the forest (pré montré). Inevitably, when it gave its name to a religious order, by a play on words it became «the field shown» to Saint Norbert or the place «foreshown» (praemonstratum or prémontré).

Although Prémontré seemed a most unattractive place and, in the first instance, it was a spiritual intuition that drew Norbert to settle there, yet it was for various reasons particularly suitable for the mother house of a great order. In spite of its secluded situation it lay close to the intersection of two important European highways – that from England to Italy through Calais and Basle, and that from Germany through Cologne to Paris and thence southwards to the Mediterranean. It was in a region where the movement of reform in the Church was at its most vigorous and in the diocese of Laon, which was part of the royal domain of the French crown, yet within easy reach of Germany, where Norbert still had influential connections. The Bishop, who was, as we have seen, a devoted admirer of Norbert, had the ears of the Pope and the King of France, to both of whom he was related. Finally it was near one of the great intellectual centres of the day, the cathedral school of Laon, which was to give several of its best men to Prémontré.

In conclusion, surely no one can read the story of Saint Norbert without echoing the words of the monk, Hermann, in admiration for «the generosity of this bishop, who set aside all his other business and put himself to so much trouble to take an unknown man round so many wild and trackless places, which even today, when they have been settled, still seem forbidding but then, when they were far removed from all human habitation, were much more savage and frightening, the haunts of wolves and wild boars.»

CHAPTER V

THE FOUNDER.

Norbert now settled at Prémontré, alone except for the one companion who still remained with him. After a few days he went back to Laon to visit the school of Ralph, not to study this time but to address the students. As a result of his talk seven young men, who had recently come from Lorraine, asked to join Norbert and went back with him to Prémontré. They were well to do and brought a large sum of money with them, which seemed a godsend to the young community since it had as yet no funds of its own. The money was entrusted to Norbert's companion for safe keeping but alas ! he disappeared during the night taking it with him, and was never seen again. The brethren were thus left destitute and suffered severe hardship. Norbert now remembered the voices that he had heard on the road near Rheims, the one saying : «Here comes Norbert with his two companions», and the other replying : «No ! Here comes Norbert with his one companion». Sad to relate the thief was an Englishman !

As soon as the worst of the winter was over, probably at the end of February, Norbert set out on one of his preaching tours. He was alone this time but hoped to gain recruits for his new foundation. When he preached at Cambrai there was among his hearers a young man, barely twenty years of age, called Evermode. As he listened it seemed to him that Christ was making a personal appeal to him to leave everything and follow Him. As soon as the sermon was finished he there and then offered himself to Norbert and was accepted. He was to become his intimate friend and to be his constant companion for the rest of his life.

Norbert was covering much the same ground as in the previous year and so he came to Nivelles, where another young man, called Anthony, joined him. After an absence of six or seven weeks he returned to Prémontré a few days before Palm Sunday, which fell on 11 April, bringing thirteen new novices with him.

It was now that he formally established the monastery at Prémontré where the community began to clear the ground and build some rough huts around the chapel. All the rest of the year 1120 and the first weeks of the following year Norbert devoted to training his young community and instructing them in the religious life. They were enthusiastic but inexperienced in spiritual matters so that it was not surprising if in these early days some of them made mistakes or even suffered delusions brought on by overexertion in spiritual exercises or too much fasting.

About the middle of February 1121 Norbert set out once more to preach during Lent, as was his custom, but we have no record of where he went this year. For the most part it seems that all went well at Prémontré while he was away. The only serious trouble was caused by Brother Gerard. He was normally an exemplary religious, prompt to obey, devout in prayer but unwise in his excessive asceticism. He insisted on fasting the whole year round, summer and winter alike, never eating more than once a day except on Sundays, and even then he would only take something uncooked, without garnishing. He was admired by everyone and his austerities became the subject of pious gossip. Then on Ash Wednesday, when everyone else began the Lenten Fast, he suddenly became ravenously hungry and said that he could not fast; that he would die if he did not have milk and cheese. When it was pointed out to him that not even layfolk were allowed more than one meal a day during Lent and that even children were bound to abstain from milk and cheese, he glared around him like a starving wolf and said that surely God did not intend that a man should die of starvation. In the absence of Norbert the brothers were sorely puzzled as to how to deal with such a case. In the end they did prevail on Brother Gerard to abstain from milk and cheese on condition that he could have two meals a day and eat as much of the Lenten foods as he wished. They were afraid of the scandal that would be caused if it became known that, in spite of the strictness of their rule, the brethren could not even remain faithful to the practices observed by ordinary christians in the world.

When Norbert returned shortly before Easter, he was overwhelmed by a feeling of depression as he entered the valley of Prémontré and he knew that something was wrong. As soon as he reached the monastery the brethren met him and, somewhat abashed, they told him in answer to his questions all that had happened. What he heard greatly saddened him, not only on account of Brother Gerard, but also because the others had shown themselves so weak and unable to deal with the situation. At once he sent for Brother Gerard but, when they brought him in, he saw that he had put on so much weight that he was scarcely recognizable. He had become such a slave to gluttony that, when he met the master to whom he had always been so devoted in the past, he could only glare at him savagely. Norbert saw that this was no ordinary case and that it must be handled firmly and yet with understanding. He ordered that he should be starved for a few days, after which he was put on a daily ration of a quarter of a loaf and a jug of water. So with God's grace he returned to a sensible and well regulated way of life.

It was about this time that a local council was held at Soissons, presided over by the papal legate for France, Conon, Cardinal Bishop of Palestrina. Its principal purpose was to examine a book on the Trinity written by Peter Abelard. He has been described as «one of the most brilliant teachers in all history and, by his use of the new logic in the study of the traditional doctrine, one of the creators of scientific theology». He was alas ! as arrogant as he was brilliant. At the council his teaching on the Trinity was condemned and he was obliged to proclaim publicly his acceptance of the Athanasian Creed. We do not know whether or not Norbert attended this council, although it is quite possible that he did, Soissons being only a short distance from Prémontré. He must, however, have been in close touch with events and Abelard certainly counted him among his enemies. In his work, «The History of My Misfortunes», he complains of «certain new apostles who rose up against me and in whom the world showed great confidence. One of them prided himself on having restored the way of life of the canons regular, the other that of the monks». The reference was plainly to Norbert and Bernard of Clairvaux. He continued to feel great bitterness towards Norbert, for he returned to the attack in a sermon in which he accuses him by name of spiritual pride and of faking miracles, even of pretending falsely to raise the dead to life.

It was during this same year, 1121, that Bishop Bartholomew took the necessary legal action to establish the new foundation and to make it secure for all time. This was embodied in two charters. The first affirmed the Bishop's right to give the property to Norbert and ran thus : «Bartholomew, by the grace of God, Bishop of Laon.

Whereas the Abbey of Saint Vincent held by gift of our predecessor, Elinand, the place commonly known as Prémontré, which used to belong to the bishopric, as is stated in the chartulary of that church; the monks having held it for a long time and worked the land with little or no profit, I asked Abbot Adalbero and the monks to transfer to me the freehold of that property, so that I could dispose of it as I might wish. As a token of my gratitude to them for their kindness I granted them the church of Berry-au-bac and half a bushel of wheat at the mill of Brancourt. Moreover, seeing that the said property of Prémontré was most suitable for a religious community, I have granted it to be held absolutely in freehold for all time by Brother Norbert and his subjects, and their successors. However Brother Norbert, in his scrupulous respect for the rights of others, was unwilling to accept the gift unless Abbot Sifrid (4) and his monks had first ratified the same gift by their common assent given in chapter. Accordingly, so that this grant may never hereafter be impugned, we have seen fit to attest it by the impression of our own seal as well as by the seal of the Church of Saint Mary of Laon and that of Sifrid, Abbot of Saint Vincent's. Given at Laon in the Chapter of the Church of Saint Mary of Laon in the year of Our Lord's Incarnation 1121».

The second was the foundation charter of the new monastery. It was a longer document giving in legal form a detailed description of the whole property which was given by Bishop Bartholomew «to Norbert a man universally respected for his piety, and to his successors persevering

---

(4) Abbot Adalbero had died and Abbot Sifrid had been elected to succeed him.

in their holy vocation... to build a church (and monastery) to the honour of God and the Holy Mother of God». There was ample land for the support of a great abbey and the Bishop included the surrounding hills in this gift. All of this was to be held free from tithes, rents and all other charges. To make sure that the religious should not be disturbed in any way, he obtained from the feudal lord of the district, Thomas de Marle, the formal renunciation of all his dues and rights in the property as well as the rights of his foresters. Finally, with the consent of all concerned, he closed the existing right of way through the valley.

From the beginning there was a very close and friendly association between Prémontré and the Abbey of Saint Vincent at Laon, which continued until both houses were suppressed in the French Revolution. When a religious of either house died the same masses and prayers were offered for him in the other as for one of its own members.

We have already seen that Laon and the surrounding district, including Prémontré, were part of the crown lands of the King of France, who was at this time Louis VI. He was a good King, a fearless champion of order and justice, a kindly man and a staunch supporter of the Church. When he visited Laon in 1121, he issued a charter at Bishop Bartholomew's request confirming the foundation of Prémontré and taking it under the protection of the crown.

Now that the new foundation was officially recognized Norbert had to think of building a permanent monastery to replace the huts but first, and most important of all, there must be a great church to which everything else must be subordinate. In those days it was considered essential that a church of any importance should be built over the tomb of a saint or at least should contain the relics of saints, which were regarded as its most precious possessions. Accordingly, when Norbert set out in the late summer or early autumn of 1121 on a preaching tour, which he hoped would bring in more recruits, he intended to include Cologne in his itinerary since that city was exceptionally well endowed with relics and, through his friendship with the Archbishop, he hoped to obtain all that would be needed for his new Church.

He had not gone far when, to his great joy, was rejoined by his first companion, Hugh of Fosses, who had now finally settled his affairs. Together they went on their way, Norbert preaching everywhere and reconciling those who had quarrelled. When they came to Nivelles they had a very hostile reception, which was surprising since Norbert had preached there the previous year with great success and had won the hearts of the people. Indeed several of them had followed the example of their compatriot, Brother Anthony, and had gone to join the new community at Prémontré. However, finding the life there much stricter than they had expected, they soon returned home, disillusioned, and to justify themselves they blackened Norbert's character. Now they refused to listen to his preaching or to have anything to do with him and did all that they could to turn the people against him. Such setbacks were nothing new to Norbert and he did not give way to discouragement, knowing that God only permits such trials for His own good purpose.

Events soon took an unexpected turn when one of the townsmen came to Norbert in great distress to ask for his help. He told him that for the past year his daughter, who was only twelve, had been tormented by an evil spirit and that sometimes she had become so violent that she had to be forcibly restrained. He was moved by the father's appeal and asked that the girl should be brought to him. By the time she arrived a crowd had gathered and Norbert proceeded with the service of exorcism while the girl mocked and ridiculed it. Then, although she had never learnt any of the Bible except a few psalms, she suddenly started to recite the whole of the Song of Songs in Latin after which she translated it word by word first into French and then into German. This done she became more defiant and aggressive than ever.

When at last the evening came Norbert was sad because he had not been able to help the girl and he asked that she should be brought back for Mass on the morrow. He had eaten nothing all day but he would not take any food for he was resolved to fast until she was cured.

In the morning the people flocked to Mass, curious to see how the affair could end. The girl continued to mock until the elevation when she shouted; «I am on fire. Let me go», and then she was at peace. She was carried back to her home in a state of utter collapse but soon, after she had eaten, she appeared none the worse for her experience and recovered completely. Norbert's reputation was thus publicly vindicated and there was universal rejoicing in the town.

It was early in October that Norbert came to Cologne, where everyone was pleased to see him. They all remembered the rich young nobleman and the circumstances of his conversion and were very curious to see what he was like now. So they flocked to hear his sermons and to go to confession to him. For the general mass of the people his visit became a nine days' wonder but there were many, both clerics and laymen, who were moved by his preaching to join him in the perfect following of Christ in His poverty.

Meanwhile Norbert approached the Archbishop and other leading churchman with his request for relics, which they considered fair and reasonable and, as the people also looked on it favourably, they had no hesitation in granting it. Accordingly Norbert ordered a day of prayer and fasting for the brethren who were with him to ask for God's blessing on their quest. The next morning they began their search and found the complete remains of one of the Virgin martyrs known as Saint Ursula and her companions who had been venerated in Cologne since the 4th century. These relics together with those of other saints were given to him in two reliquaries during a solemn service of thanksgiving.

On the following day, which was 12 October, he went to the Provost and Canons of the Collegiate Church of Saint Gereon the Martyr and asked them for some relics of their saint. The place of his burial had long been forgotten and they gave him permission to search in their church, saying that he would be welcome to take whatever he might find. Norbert, who was delighted, spent the whole night in prayer, commending his venture to God. We have an eyewitness account of the search by Rudolph, an abbot who was present as the Archbishop's representative. He tells us that a number of members of the clergy, including some monks and abbots, were there, praying and helping to dig. Suddenly Norbert directed their attention to a spot in the middle of the monastery where there was no indication that any burial had ever taken place. They began to dig and soon, to everyone's surprise, they found a body which had obviously been laid there with the greatest care in a sarcophagus that was covered, almost at ground level, by a thin slab of marble. The body had been wrapped in a green material which had perished with age, whilst on the cloak there was a large cross above the breast, embroidered in gold thread. This, with the military boots and spurs, showed that it was the body of a soldier. (Saint Gereon had been an officer in the Roman Army). The upper part of the head was missing and between the body and the bottom of the sarcophagus there had been placed turfs soaked in the martyr's blood. The canons were overjoyed at this discovery as was the immense crowd that had gathered. The holiday mood spread among the people of Cologne and Norbert became the hero of the hour. There could be no doubt that the body which he had found was that of their patron, Saint Gereon, which had been completely lost for many years and which, search as they might, neither the canons nor their predecessors had ever been able to find. The history of the martyrdom of Saint Gereon relates that the sword of the executioner severed the upper part of the head above the chin and that the pagans had thrown it into a well. This had been recovered and was enshrined in the church but the burial place of the rest of the body had been forgotten until now.

Norbert's popularity was short-lived for soon the rumour went around that he was going to take the relics away with him and the crowd was in a turmoil. The disturbance was quietened with some difficulty and, to pacify the people, the Archbishop ordered that the grave should be sealed and guarded until permanent arrangements could be made but, before doing so, he had given Norbert part of the relics.

Shortly after this, towards the end of October, Norbert set out on his return journey with the clerics and laymen who had asked to join him, taking the relics with him.

As they approached Namur the Countess, Ermensinde by name, having heard that he was coming that way, came to meet Norbert. She told him that she and the Count possessed a small church in the valley of Sambre, some six or seven miles South West of Namur, where it had long been her desire to found a monastery. She begged him to accept it and settle some of his brethren there and he, impressed by her sincerity, agreed to her request. The necessary legal formalities were completed very quickly and on 21 November Count Godfrey and the Countess, with the consent of their children signed the deed conveying the Church of Our Lady at Floreffe to Norbert, his brothers and their successors, together with an ample endowment for the support of the monastery. Norbert left a small community to make the new foundation and gave them one of the two reliquaries. Then he hastened on his way to Prémontré, where he arrived just before Christmas, bringing with him thirty new novices, both clerics and laybrothers.

CHAPTER VI

THE WHITE CANONS.

By the end of 1121 the community at Prémontré consisted of some forty clerics and a large number of laybrothers. All were still novices and Norbert used to assemble them every morning and evening to encourage them in their resolve as well as to instruct them in the duties of the religious life and in the meaning of the vows that they were to make. They were immensely impressed by the depth of his spirituality and the utter unworldliness of his teaching but, more than anything that he said, it was the living example of Norbert himself that was their inspiration.

Many of the brethren came to have such confidence in his teaching and spiritual direction that they saw no need for any formal rule. Norbert, however, was well aware that no institution which was entirely dependent on the personal leadership of one man could survive for long once the first fervour of its members had begun to cool. He warned them that without a written rule and a fixed way of life of the kind traditional in the Church it was impossible to observe perfectly the Gospel counsels and the teaching of the Apostles. The brethren readily accepted his advice and said that they would be guided by whatever he might decide in the matter of a rule. Realizing, as he did, the tremendous responsibility that their confidence imposed on him, he knew that this was not a decision to be made lightly. In fact the question as to what should be the character and way of life of the community that he was founding had been on his mind for some time. He had received all kinds of advice from bishops and abbots. Some urged him to adopt a secluded contemplative life, or even to found a community of hermits, whilst others suggested that he should seek incorporation into the Cistercian Order. Moreover he could draw on his own fairly extensive first hand experience of the life of various religious communities. He was, however, firmly convinced that the new foundation did not owe its origin to him nor to any other man but to God alone, to Whose grace he attributed whatever success had so far attended this undertaking and gave long and careful consideration to the problem but, above all, he sought God's guidance in prayer.

The choice may have been difficult but in one respect it was much simpler than it would be in our day. There was not the vast diversity of religious orders and congregations by which the Church is enriched today. At that time there were two main kinds of religious – the monks and the canons regular. The monks sought Christian perfection by living in community apart from the world, dividing their time between prayer, reading and work. The first monks were not priests and the priesthood has never been essential to the monastic state. Canons regular, on the other hand, are by definition priests (or candidates for the priesthood) who have adopted the religious life as a means of perfection in their priestly life and ministry. From an early date the clergy attached to a cathedral or other large church, whose life was regulated by the «canones» or decrees of the Church, had come to be known as «canonici» or canons (5). It was only to be

(5) Apparently the term «canonici» originally meant the clergy whose names were on the «canon» or register of a church.

expected that they would be influenced by the example of the monks and make use of the means of sanctification that they saw to be so efficacious in the monastic life. Thus Saint Augustine, when he became Bishop of Hippo in 396, established in his cathedral clergy house what he called a «monastery for the clergy», but his initiative did not survive him. The next landmark was when Saint Chrodegang Bishop of Metz from 746 to 766, introduced the common life for his cathedral clergy and wrote a rule for them that was widely adopted elsewhere. Then in 817 came the Rule of the Council of Aachen which was made obligatory for canons throughout the Frankish Empire. These rules exercised a beneficial influence but both had one serious defect. Although they imposed community life and required the revenues of the cathedral or collegiate church to be held in common, they allowed the canons to keep their own private property. This meant that they could enrich themselves by acquiring benefices and, in the course of time, it even became customary for them to divide the revenues of their church among themselves as prebends and to live in separate houses.

During the two centuries between about 850 and 1050 the Church passed through some bad times. Simony became prevalent, discipline was relaxed and even the law of clerical celibacy was widely disregarded. Often priests had only a rudimentary knowledge of their religion and the pastoral care of their flocks was sadly neglected.

It was to remedy these evils that the Synod of Rome in 1059 decreed that all priests, deacons and subdeacons should live in clergy houses attached to their churches. Further, it recommended that they should adopt full community life, renouncing all private property and taking the same vow of poverty as the monks. It was not to be expected that this recommendation would be welcome to all, but the clergy of many cathedrals and other churches did accept it. They became known as canons regular whilst those who retained their own property were termed secular canons. The inspiration for this reform came from two texts of Scripture. The first was Our Lord's instruction to His Apostles when «he sent them out to proclaim the Kingdom of God and to heal». He said to them, «Take nothing for the journey : neither staff, nor haversack, nor bread, nor money; and let none of you take a spare tunic». (Lk. 9,2-3). The second was from the Acts of the Apostles : «The whole group of believers were united, heart and soul; no one claimed for his own use anything that he had, as everything that they owned was held in common». (Acts 4,32). It was in the description of the life of the Apostles and their converts, given here and in several similar passages in the Acts, that the canons regular found their ideal. Like the Apostles they would «devote themselves to prayer and to the service of the word». (Acts 6,3). The movement spread rapidly and, besides the existing chapters of canons which thus adopted the full religious life, numerous other communities were specially founded for those who felt called to combine the priestly and religious lives.

It now became necessary to find a rule for the canons regular and it is not surprising that, after some false starts, they should have turned to Saint Augustine since their aim was to live the same kind of life that he had lived with his clergy. The Rule of Saint Augustine as we know it today was taken from a letter written to a community of nuns and was adapted for men shortly afterwards, possibly by the saint himself. It contains no precise or detailed regulations but is a short treatise containing all that is essential to the religious life in community. It is, therefore, flexible and adaptable to all kinds of circumstances.

In most manuscripts from the 6th to the 12th century there is prefixed to the Rule as an integral part of it a set of detailed practical regulations, known as the «Disciplina (or Ordo) Monasterii», but from the beginning of the 12th century at the latest its attribution to Saint Augustine began to be disputed. It is very brief and laconic, covering only a single page. It opens with a few words of exhortation to the love of God and one's neighbour and then it prescribes an archaic form of the Divine Office. The brethren are to fast every day throughout the year with the only meal at 3-0 p.m. Apart from three hours' reading in the afternoon the whole day outside the times of prayer is to be occupied with manual labour, and perpetual silence is to be observed. This regime may have been tolerable in the climate of North Africa but it was quite impossible in Northern Europe and was, moreover, incompatible with any active priestly ministry. Nevertheless the canons regular in many places, particularly in the North of France and in Germany, tried to observe it and it did not fall out of use completely until about 1150. In other places it was never accepted and, when in 1118 the canons of Springiersbach referred their difficulties to him, Pope Gelasius II replied expressing his doubts as to its authenticity and telling them to conform to the current usage in the Divine Office as well as to modify the prescriptions on fasting and manual labour to suit their own circumstances. This was the position as Norbert found it and the communities with which he was most familiar were those which accepted the Disciplina as part of the Rule.

As we have seen, Norbert prayed much and thought deeply about the future of Prémontré. So at last his prayers were answered and he saw clearly what was to be the vocation of himself and his followers. They were not called to be monks and, since he and those with him who were already clerics had been secular canons from their earliest years, the life of perfection for them must be that of the canons regular. For his own part his whole desire was to imitate the life of the Apostles and he had heard that Saint Augustine had been the first to restore and organize this way of life in the Church. Accordingly he asked that a copy of the Rule of Saint Augustine should be brought to him. This was done and the text which was presented to him included the Disciplina Monasterii. After he had studied it carefully he remarked that brief as it was it set forth admirably everything that was necessary for the religious life. In particular in its reference to renouncing private property it used the words : «for we wish to live the life of the Apostles», which exactly expressed his intention.

Accordingly on Christmas Day in the year 1121 Norbert and his companions made their vows and a new religious order, that of the Canons Regular of Prémontré, came into existence. Each in his turn read out the formula of profession and, having signed it, placed it on the altar. It went like this : «I, brother N., offer and give myself to the Church of Holy Mary, Mother of God, (i.e. that of Prémontré) and promise the conversion of my ways and stability in this place according to the Gospel of Christ and the precepts of the Apostles and according to the Rule of the Blessed Augustine. I promise also perfect obedience in Christ to Norbert, superior of the afore-mentioned church, and to his successors». Although they were not specifically mentioned the vows of poverty and chastity were implicitly included by virtue of the Rule.

The decision to adopt the Rule of Saint Augustine, far from solving all their problems, immediately involved

Norbert and the brethren in controversies that soon produced a serious crisis in the life of the community. The source of the trouble lay in the identification of the Disciplina Monasterii as the authentic Augustinian Rule and in Norbert's determination that it should be observed to the letter. His critics among those canons regular who did not accept it said that the text which he took to be the Rule was so brief and obscure as to be useless and that, in any case, it was spurious. Admittedly it was old but certainly it could not be the work of Saint Augustine. Moreover experience had proved that the burden it imposed was beyond endurance. Above all they insisted that there could be no conceivable justification for adopting a form of the Divine Office which was completely at variance with any rite approved by the Church.

Worst of all was the unrest within the community itself. The brethren became disturbed and unsettled as differences of opinion arose amongst them about the interpretation of the Rule. Everyone had his own ideas and was sure that he was right. They were troubled because the text of the Rule that they were following appeared to be incompatible with the practice of other religious communities. The situation became so serious that it seemed as though the young society, which was not yet firmly rooted, might fail to survive the storm.

Faced with this crisis Norbert assembled the community and addressed them. He told them they ought not to be surprised or perplexed since God's ways are always those of mercy and truth. Customs and observances may differ or change but always the bond of mutual charity, which is love, remains unchanged. The Rule itself says : «First of all let us love God and then our neighbour». It is not external practices that lead us into the Kingdom of God but the keeping of His commandments. For the rest, he told them, the Rule covered everything that was necessary to regulate the day to day life of the monastery.

CHAPTER VII

DAILY LIFE IN THE MONASTERY.

The regime at Prémontré in these early years was one of extreme austerity, as strict as that of the Trappists in our day, but the enthusiasm of Norbert's first companions was equal to the most exacting demands. Absolute silence was observed everywhere and at all times; obedience was always prompt and unquestioning; they all had a great love of poverty because Christ had been poor and they liked to wear old patched habits. Unlike other canons, who wore linen garments with black cloaks, the canons of Prémontré wore white habits of coarse woollen material and white cloaks (from which they came to be known in England as the White Canons). (6) Norbert explained that the white colour was appropriate for canons and for those who preach the Gospel, whilst woollen habits were the traditional dress of those dedicated to a life of penance. He insisted, however, that in church and for religious services linen surplices or rochets should always be worn for the sake of reverence and cleanliness.

The canons' day was divided between prayer, study, and work. The first place in the life of the community

(6) They are also known as the Premonstratensians or the Norbertines and have the suffix O. Praem. after their names. Other new orders at this time also wore white habits (e.g. the Carthusians and the Cistercians), which they adopted for no other reason than that undyed wool was the cheapest material available.

was held by the public worship of God. At midnight they rose for the Night Office after which they slept until dawn when they sang Prime followed by the Morning Mass, which was offered for the faithful departed. They returned to the church in the middle of the morning for Terce, High Mass and Sext; after dinner about 3.00 p.m. for None; in the late afternoon for Vespers and finally before retiring to rest for Compline. They met daily in chapter after the morning Mass when the Abbot might deliver a homily, any necessary business would be transacted, duties allotted and faults against the Rule corrected. Manual labour had an important place in their daily routine. Indeed Norbert had originally wanted them to be entirely dependent on it for their livelihood but his friend, Bishop Bartholomew, dissuaded him. There was, however, one kind of work which had an immense importance before the invention of printing – namely the copying of manuscripts – and the canons who did this work were exempt from manual labour and certain other duties. As in all monasteries at this period an appreciable time was set apart every day, and more on Sundays and holidays, for meditative and prayerful spiritual reading. What was distinctive of the White Canons, however, was the high value that they set on study. Every house had its librarian and special provision was made for lectures and systematic courses on such subjects as scripture and theology. The abbeys of the Order were, in fact, the first seminaries to exist in the Catholic Church for the training of parish priests.

At first they tried to live strictly according to the Disciplina Monasterii in the belief that it was the Rule of Saint Augustine, which they were vowed to observe, but within a few years it had to be abandoned and replaced by appropriate statutes. The rule about fasting had to be modified quite early because it was found to be more than human nature could endure. As to the Divine Office, in 1126 Pope Honorius II ordered that Prémontré should adopt the same rite as other religious communities. The rule of silence lasted somewhat longer, although provision had to be made in the statutes for a parlour where the brethren were allowed to speak when necessary. We have already seen that manual labour had to be substantially reduced but it continued to have its place in the life of the canons as a valuable discipline.

A casual visitor in these early years might have been pardoned if he took the canons of Prémontré for monks since their life differed little in externals from that of the Cistercians, although the nature and purpose of the two institutions were quite different. The resemblance was to be accentuated because the earliest statutes of the Order were largely borrowed from those of the Cistercians and, like the little that is still extant of Norbert's instructions to his brethren, are entirely concerned with their life inside the monastery. Their active ministry was left to develop according to circumstances; it was Norbert's intention that his canons should be ready for any kind of priestly work demanded by the needs of the Church and of souls. His way was that later to be described by Saint Thomas Aquinas as «to contemplate and to pass on to others the fruits of that contemplation» (contemplare et contemplata aliis tradere). The life of prayer and union with God was to be so full that it overflowed to enrich the world. Norbert was above all a man of prayer, a contemplative, but his life of prayer always found its outward expression in his burning love of souls.

We have seen how he went out in Lent and in the summer on his missionary journeys, preaching to all manner of men and women, in monasteries, villages and towns. Many of the layfolk who heard him were converted not just to a better life in the world but to a dedicated life of religious perfection, so that men and women flocked to Prémontré and his other foundations begging for admission. They came from all social classes but almost all were illiterate since in those days few apart from the clergy could read.

The nucleus of the community was the canons, some forty or so in number, of whom about fifteen would be priests, the rest deacons and subdeacons. There were between four and five hundred laybrothers, whose quarters were separate from those of the canons. Since they could not read they recited a fixed number of Our Fathers instead of the Office and on weekdays were present in the church only for Matins, the Morning Mass and Compline. The rest of the day they spent working with their hands and there was plenty to occupy them – clearing the forest, draining the marshes, farming the land and carrying on all the trades required to support a self-sufficient community. On the other side of the church from the monastery was the convent where more than a thousand sisters lived. Many of them had held good positions in the world, some even belonged to the highest aristocracy, but all alike were happy as simple laysisters, working at such tasks as helping in the dairy and the garden, spinning and sewing or doing anything else that might be necessary. Their religious exercises were the same as those of the laybrothers.

Outside the gates of the monastery Norbert founded a hostel which fulfilled three functions – first as a guest house where any traveller would find a welcome, secondly as a hospice where the poor were given food and shelter and thirdly as a hospital for the sick. The men were looked after by the canons and the laybrothers and the women by the sisters.

The priests in the community were responsible for the administration of this large establishment as well as the pastoral care and spiritual direction of the brothers, the sisters, and the poor and the sick in the hostel. In addition some of them always went out with Norbert on his missionary tours to help in the work. Lastly there were the beginnings of what was to become the characteristic work of the White Canons, the serving of parishes. Although most of the houses in the early days were founded in secluded situations, there were from the start some foundations in cities, such as Saint Martin's at Laon and Saint Michael's at Antwerp, where the canons had the care of souls and later, when Norbert went to Magdeburg as archbishop, he entrusted several parishes to his canons. In the course of time all the abbeys of the Order came to have parishes served by their priests. Meanwhile Prémontré and the other houses had farms (or granges as they were called) at some distance from the monastery where laybrothers lived and worked the land. The canons would say Mass for them and in due course residences were established where two or three of them would live together. They became centres round which the country people would settle and build villages and in this way parishes would develop served by the canons.

Norbert's ideal was expressed well by Abbot Hugo, O. Praem., writing in 1704 : «He gave his children as their aim to work with the grace of God for the salvation and perfection of their souls. He joined to this the work of preaching and sanctifying their neighbours, being convinced that nothing contributes more to our own sanctification than to devote ourselves to the salvation of souls, and that nothing fits us better to save souls than sanctifying ourselves. In his institute he associated silence and the austerities of the monastic life with the duties of the clerical life. From the former he took prayer, retirement, self denial and the singing of the Divine Office; from the latter preaching, missionary work, serving parishes and the study of scripture and theology without which it is impossible to exercise the Gospel ministry. This was what he had in mind when he fixed the formula for their profession which all made with him on Christmas Day in the year 1121».

It must not be imagined that in such a large community human weakness and human failings could be absent. Some of the brethren tended to become slack and negligent, others were wanting in courage and generosity and there were a few rebellious spirits, but all alike found in Norbert a wise and understanding superior, although when necessary he could be severe in his reprimands. His spiritual teaching was simple and based on the fundamental principles of the religious life. His whole endeavour was to empty the hearts of his followers of self so that they should be open to God and to the working of the Holy Spirit. He impressed on them that they must renounce themselves and all that they possessed, purely for the love of God, and that they must take up the cross every day by a life of penance; that is to say by a patient acceptance of the many trials and sufferings of daily life. He laid special stress on the evangelical counsels of prompt obedience, voluntary poverty and perfect chastity which, he said, constitute the very essence of the Order without which it could not survive. He warned them of the danger to their spiritual lives of excessive involvement in external activities and he urged them to keep a watch over their tongues so as to avoid grumbling, detraction and spiteful talk. They should be united in mutual charity so that, in the words of the Rule, «they should have but one heart and mind in the house of God». He assured them that they had nothing to fear as long as they remained faithful to their vow to strive to live by the Gospel, the teaching of the Apostles and the Rule of Saint Augustine, which embodied it. There was one phrase which summed up the whole way of life taught by Norbert : «to follow the sacred scriptures and to have Christ as leader».

Among the traditional practices of the canons there were three that he had particularly at heart and never ceased to commend most insistently to his followers – the public worship of God, the correction of faults and the practice of hospitality. Liturgical worship had always been the first duty of canons and he used to insist that in the church and at religious services everything should be clean and tidy. He attached the greatest importance to correcting faults not only in chapter but whenever the occasion arose. He knew that without a constant effort at self-improvement slackness creeps in and eventually infects the whole community. Norbert's heart was always open to the needs of others and he set great store by hospitality, especially the care of the sick and the poor. «At the altar», he used to say, «one shows one's faith and love of God; in purifying one's conscience one's care for oneself; in welcoming guests and the poor one's love for one's neighbour». He never tired of saying that any house that was faithful in these three matters would never be permitted to suffer want beyond what it could bear.

To conclude, an interesting light is thrown on the choice of the Rule of Saint Augustine by something that Norbert later told to the community of Kappenberg, a house that was especially dear to him. One of those who heard him recorded what he said in these words : «I heard him speaking in chapter as follows : 'I know,' he said, 'one of the brethren of our society who was deep in thought as to what our rule should be when, not through any merits of his own but in answer to the prayers of his brothers, Saint Augustine appeared to him. He took his Golden Rule, which he had brought, and offered it to him. At the same time, speaking clearly, he made himself known, saying : «I, whom you see, am Augustine, Bishop of Hippo. Here you have the rule which I wrote. Your brothers, my sons, if they serve under it loyally will stand before Christ without fear on the terrible day of the last judgement'. Although his humility made him speak as though of someone else, we had no doubt at all that it was to him that the revelation was made.»

CHAPTER VIII

THE BEGINNINGS OF THE ORDER.

New Year's day 1122 found the large and rapidly growing community at Prémontré still living in the huts which they had built round the tiny chapel of Saint John the Baptist. Plainly an immediate decision had to be made about the site and plans of the church and the permanent conventual buildings. We have already seen how marshy and inhospitable the valley was and now the brethren, almost without exception, began to remonstrate about its total unsuitability as the site of a monastery; nor were the people of the neighbourhood backward in supporting their view that no foundation could last long in such a barren wilderness. Norbert himself never faltered or lost confidence but he saw that, if his little flock was not to lose heart completely, he must do something to encourage them and silence his detractors. Accordingly he set out to examine all the possibilities of the place and told others to do likewise, at the same time ordering special prayers to be said for God's guidance. The whole community prayed fervently, offering their fasting and self-denial for this intention, and then one day a brother came to tell Norbert of a vision. In the centre of the valley, where another valley intersected it at right angles, he had plainly seen Our Lord on the cross but radiant in the light of seven sunbeams of amazing brightness. From the four quarters of the world there came, hastening along these valleys, an immense multitude of pilgrims with wallets and staffs. They knelt in adoration of their Redeemer and kissed His feet. Then they departed as thought sent out on a mission, each one returning along the way by which he had come. When Norbert heard this his face lit up with joy and he thanked God. Any misgivings that he may have had vanished and he told the brethren that they should take courage in their warfare against the forces of evil for this vision was clearly prophetic of the recruits who would come to join them in Christ's service and fight by their side until the end of time.

The site of the church being thus decided, the work was put in hand without delay but no sooner had the workmen begun to dig for the foundations than they struck a snag that threatened to prove fatal to the whole project. The ground was found to be so marshy that any attempt to build on it seemed quite hopeless. It was only with the greatest difficulty, by emptying countless loads of stone into the excavations, that they eventually succeeded in making a firm base for the structure. Meanwhile a date had been fixed for the solemn blessing of the foundation stones and Bishop Bartholomew was invited to perform the ceremony.

On the appointed day he came with Bishop Lisiard of Soissons, also a friend of Norbert, and there was a large gathering of the leading churchmen and laity as well as a vast crowd of ordinary people. Recent events had aroused a great deal of interest in the district and they had come to see everything for themselves. What sort of a man could this Norbert be, they asked ? Surely he must be a man of great faith – more faith, indeed, than common sense ! they wondered how any lasting success could be expected in such a remote wilderness or any buildings stand firm in such a quagmire.

None of the names of the important people who were present has come down to us except that of Thomas de Marle, Lord of Courcy, who came with his small son, Engelrand. His presence on such an occasion may have seemed somewhat surprising for, even among the robber barons of that age, he was notorious for his wickedness. He «took a perverted delight in cruelty for its own sake, ... tortured and murdered unoffending peasants, robbed and imprisoned merchants and made his name a by-word for inhumanity». (b) On one occasion he was excommunicated and a crusade preached against him but still he did not mend his ways. Yet he feared Norbert and held him in respect as a man of God. His son never forgot this day and grew up to become a great benefactor of Prémontré.

Once begun the work went ahead with astonishing speed for some of Norbert's friends at Cologne had hired German masons and there was keen rivalry between them and the local men. The Germans built one side of the church and the French the other, each group striving for all that they were worth to outbuild the other. In this way the church was completed and ready to be consecrated within nine months.

The day of the consecration began with much rejoicing among the many visitors who had come, some of them from great distances, to witness the ceremony but alas ! it ended in a sad disappointment. Everything went well until the offertory, when the tightly packed crowd was pressing forward towards the sanctuary to make their offerings and walk round the high altar as was then customary. Suddenly the heavy altar began to slip, the

(b) «A History of Europe from 911 to 1198» by Z.N. Brooke, p. 296.

stone cracked and broke and thus the whole ceremony was rendered invalid. Norbert was dismayed and saddened but, most of all, he feared the scandal that might be caused among the weaker and more superstitious spirits, although he himself had complete trust in God's providence. Accordingly he arranged with the Bishop that he should come back to consecrate the church and the new altar on 18 November, the octave day of Saint Martin. The accident to the altar left a lasting impression on Norbert and it was the occasion of a strange premonition. He saw in it a sign that in future times there would have to be a great renewal and for the rest of his life he often spoke about it. Indeed the Order almost did become extinct after the French Revolution but since then it has known an amazing revival.

The church, which was dedicated to Our Lady, was one of the finest Romanesque churches in France and remained the mother church of the Order for more than six and a half centuries but, sadly, all that remains of it today are some ruins. The rest of the conventual buildings were not completed by Norbert during his time at Prémontré but by Hugh of Fosses, who took over from him. A contemporary writer and near neighbour, the monk Hermann of Laon, wrote of Prémontré that «among the richest and most ancient religious houses of France it would be hard to find its equal» and tells us that it always gave Bishop Bartholomew immense joy to visit it.

Norbert had not remained at Prémontré while the church was being built but had gone out on another of his missionary journeys, leaving Hugh of Fosses in charge. Before he left he appointed officials to be responsible for every department of the life and work of the monastery and had taken the precaution of having an alternate holder for each office. Before taking his leave he spoke to them on the importance of preserving peace and charity among themselves, saying that no community would come to harm as long as its superiors remained united.

No sooner had Norbert gone on his way this time than the community began to be plagued by an outbreak of psychic disturbances. This is, perhaps, not surprising since many of the recent arrivals had more good will and enthusiasm than experience or training in the religious life and the men of that age were only too ready to look for the tangible or visible intervention of demons in their lives. On one occasion, in the full light of day, some of the brethren became convinced that they could hear the clash of arms and the neighing of horses and picked up sticks and stones to defend themselves against the attacks of their enemies. The others, who heard the disturbance, came running up to see what was happening; they tried to calm them and bring them back to their senses, but without success for, believing that they were victorious, they now rushed off in pursuit of their imaginary enemy, shouting threats. When eventually they returned to reality and saw that they had been the victims of an hallucination, some, frankly recognizing their error, firmly resolved never to fall into the same trap again but others, unable to bear the shame of being tricked like this, gave way to despair and abandoned their vocation.

Then some of the young clerics who were indifferent scholars and, indeed, could only read with difficulty suddenly began to comment on the most difficult parts of the Bible and to make astonishing prophecies about future events. There was one who claimed to understand the Book of Daniel and explained the passage about the horned beasts, the kings and Anti-Christ so plausibly that he gained a following among the simpler brethren and almost succeeded in deceiving the learned Abbot Simon of Saint

Nicholas at Laon. One day, when they were present in the chapter house, he had the effrontery to get up and begin to preach on the text : «Be valiant in war and fight against the ancient serpent», but when he came to the words : «And you will win the everlasting kingdom», he suddenly found himself unable to say another word. In spite of this setback he was in no way discouraged but shortly afterwards, during Norbert's absence, he seemed to be seriously ill. Now as he lay in the infirmary, he began to speak about heaven and the mysteries of the unseen world to the community, who had gathered round his bed to assist at his anointing and to hear his last words. He said that on that very evening he would be with the angels in heaven. Then he went on to make even more sensational prophecies about some of those present. He said that he had just been rapt in ecstasy and had seen one of them called to eternal life and another in heaven, such a one would be a bishop, another the teacher and superior of many religious, this one would persevere in his vocation and that other would abandon it. After he had spoken he seemed to be at the point of death and lay motionless for the space of an hour. Then, at the first sound of the bell for vespers, he rose and hurried to join the others in the church. When they saw this they had to admit, with a feeling of shame, that they had been fooled.

Another cleric, Reynald by name, an ignorant man who had never studied the scriptures, claimed that, during a nightlong ecstasy, an angel had explained the mysteries of the Book of Revelation to him. Word of this was brought to one of the superiors while the brethren were at work and he assembled them to hear the visionary expound his message, but they had learned their lesson and refused to listen to him or anyone else until Norbert should return.

A bitter feud arose between this brother and a rival, called Burchard, and their mutual animosity became so fierce that they had to be forcibly restrained to prevent their violently assaulting each other. As they sat facing one another Reynald was flushed with rage while Burchard wept bitterly. When asked the cause of his grief he sobbed out that his enemy was plotting his death and that, if they searched his bed, they would find the evidence. The beds of both were searched and hidden in one was found a long knife and in the other a heavy club, which were produced before the community. The prior took advantage of the occasion to deliver a stern homily and to impose silence on them all until Norbert's return. Thereafter they were on their guard even more than before.

Meanwhile Norbert had gone northward into the province of Brabant, his first objective being Floreffe, where on 25th January, the Feast of Saint Paul's Conversion, the new monastery founded in November, when he was on his way back from Cologne, was inaugurated and the community, which was drawn from Prémontré, took formal possession. We do not know whether Norbert was present at the ceremony but, if not, he certainly arrived shortly afterwards and stayed long enough to see the new foundation firmly established. Floreffe, the eldest daughter of Prémontré, was to have a great future, not that any of its religious were to become famous, but for nearly seven centuries, except for a few years in the 14th century, it was to maintain such a high standard of observance that it never needed reform and was to give the Church countless zealous and devoted parish priests.

Leaving Floreffe he continued his journey to Namur, Huy, Liège, Tongres and other towns, including perhaps Louvain, but we have no record of his activities until he came to Maastricht, where he arrived in time for the feast of its patron saint on 13 May. He celebrated mass that day before a large congregation in the principal church of the town. Immediately after mass, as he was leaving the altar, they brought up to him a young man, the bailiff of a nobleman, who was, they said, possessed by an evil spirit and whom they begged him to heal. He was shouting and struggling so violently that they had the greatest difficulty in holding him but Norbert agreed to their request and began the service of exorcism immediately. In the late afternoon some of the brethren, seeing how exhausted he was, wanted him to take some rest for the sake of his health but he firmly refused, warning them that the evil one never rests in his warfare against souls. Clergy and layfolk had gathered to watch, some out of piety, others out of curiosity, and then, as they stood around, the young man started to speak about the sinful lives of many of them, their adultery and immorality, all the secret sins that they had not mentioned in confession. As he spoke they slipped out one by one until only a few were left. At last when it was becoming dark they insisted that Norbert should retire to the guest house to restore his strength with food and sleep. While he was sitting at supper with his brethren and a few guests news was brought that the sick man had recovered and was sitting quietly in front of the altar and that he was asking pardon for all the wicked things that he had said. They all thanked God and, indeed, for the whole of that night and the next day he appeared to be cured. Norbert was occupied all that day working to reconcile the townsmen, who were divided by a murderous feud. When he returned in the evening, however, he was met with the news that the poor young man was worse than ever, shouting and raging, and that, unless something was done at once to cure him, he would make away with himself. Norbert did not agree and said that nothing could be done for him yet, since his sufferings had been brought on by his own sins. (He had, it seems, been misusing his office as bailiff). He should be left to himself for a few days and then, his offences being expiated, he could be cured. In the event, after three days of acute suffering, he was healed by Norbert and went back home in perfect health of mind and body.

That year Norbert broke new ground, crossing the Rhine into Westphalia, and no sooner was his arrival known than he received a visit from one of the most important nobles of the province, Count Godfrey of Kappenberg. The count was a very wealthy man, possessing wide estates with many serfs and having a large body of retainers. He was of the highest aristocracy, descended from ducal families through both his father and mother and was even related to the Emperor. He was married to Jutta, daughter of the rich and powerful Count Frederick of Arnsberg. He was at this date twenty years of age, a young man of great personal charm and immense kindliness and generosity, a fine natural speaker with bright, sparkling eyes. He did not forget the poor and it is related how, on one of his daily visits to a beggar who was receiving his hospitality, he astonished his attendants by putting the man's filthy bowl to his lips. Deeply religious as he was he had been greatly impressed by all that he had heard about Norbert, whose reputation had spread far and wide. Before this meeting he had heard Norbert speak, probably at Cologne the previous year, and had become convinced that he was not doing enough for God and that he was called to enter the religious life. As may be imagined, when he announced that he proposed to offer himself with all that he possessed to the Church he met with the most formidable opposition. All his vassals and retainers, and even his servants, objected strongly for they could not understand how a man who had everything the world could offer and to whom they were devoted could throw it all away; but the strongest opposition came, not unnaturally, from his wife and his younger brother Otto. It seemed that there was no possibility of arriving at any agreement but at last Godfrey's arguments proved to be so persuasive that both his wife and his brother were won over completely to his views and decided to enter the religious life themselves. So it came about that, as soon as he heard of Norbert's approach, he went to see him and confided all his thoughts and aspirations to him, saying that he was resolved to give up everything forthwith and embrace voluntary poverty. He said that he had made up his mind to offer himself and all his possessions to God through Norbert if the castle of Kappenberg could be converted into a monastery. Norbert accepted his offer and, since the preliminary arrangements had already been made, it was possible to complete the legal formalities so quickly that the deed of transfer was signed on 31 May. The work of adapting the castle as a religious house was put in hand at once and on 15 August, the feast of the Assumption of Our Lady, the Bishop of Münster came and, in spite of his frankly expressed doubts about the wisdom of Count Godfrey's plan, he blessed the monastery and the temporary church.

Kappenberg was always peculiarly dear to Norbert, who was its first provost, (as the superiors of the Order were called in Germany), and retained this office to the end of his life. He seemed to find it easy to speak freely to the community there and to confide in them. It was to them that he spoke of having received the Rule from Saint Augustine himself and on one occasion he told them how in a vision he had seen the Holy Spirit descending on the place, whilst on another he had seen the whole mountain illuminated supernaturally by a brilliant light.

Kappenberg was colonised from Prémontré, as were two other houses founded about the same time (1122-1123), and all three, like many of Norbert's foundations, were double monasteries with a convent of sisters close to the church. At Kappenberg the convent was at the foot of the hill and was known as the Niederkloster, and it was here that Jutta entered religion. The other two monasteries were respectively at Varlar in the diocese of Münster on a property given by Otto and at Ilbenstadt across the Rhine in the diocese of Mainz where the estate was jointly owned by the two brothers. In their charters approving the foundation of Varlar and Ilbenstadt the bishops specifically authorized the canons to exercise a pastoral ministry in the district, whilst a few years later Pope Innocent II entrusted the whole province to the care of the canons of Ilbenstadt.

On Norbert's advice Count Godfrey did not take the habit immediately but remained in the world for the time being in order to be able to assist more effectively in making the new foundation secure in the face of all the difficulties and dangers by which it was beset.

The greatest danger was from his father-in-law, Count Frederick of Arnsberg, who had become his implacable enemy. A man of overweening ambition, he wanted to get possession of the castle of Kappenberg, which being situated on a steep hill was virtually impregnable and dominated the surrounding country for a considerable distance. He falsely claimed that it was part of his daughter's dowry and threatened the community that, unless they left it quickly, he would have them all put to death. It was not without good reason that he had been nicknamed «the Warrior» and it was no idle threat that he made. Several times he approached the castle with his knights and he publicly proclaimed that, if he laid hands on Norbert, he would hang him and his ass from the same beam to see which was the heavier. When he repeated his threat at an assembly of bishops and nobles, they rebuked him and warned him to beware of the wrath of God. (Norbert was held in the highest regard throughout the Rhineland and they would not tolerate his being threatened or insulted). Count Godfrey remained calm and said that, if he should be made prisoner, word was to be sent to Norbert not to go to any trouble to secure his release. He was ready, if need be, to die for his cause. He was quite fearless as was shown when Jutta was kidnapped by a ruffian sent by her father. As soon as he heard of it Godfrey set off in pursuit and caught up with the man who drew his sword to attack him. Godfrey did not say a word but offered his neck to the would-be murderer, which so disconcerted him that he quietly slunk away.

At length Count Frederick came and laid siege to the castle so that the brethren, seeing no hope of relief, made their confessions and prepared to meet their end. They had, however, been able to send a message to Norbert to let him know of their predicament and of the Count's threats. As soon as he received it he set out on his donkey to go and face Count Frederick. He crossed the Rhine and came into the Count's territory alone and defenceless, but while he was still on his way the danger was unexpectedly removed, for one day as the Count sat at table he suffered a sudden rupture of his bowels and died in agony a short time later.

It was during this same year, 1123, while the threat from Count Frederick was at its height, that Norbert had gone with Godfrey to seek the Emperor's support. This had been possible because Henry V was at last reconciled with the Church as a result of the Concordat of Worms concluded on 23 September, 1122. Henry had recognized the right of the Church to elect bishops freely and had given up his claim to invest them with ring and crozier, whilst the Pope had agreed that the elections should take place in the presence of the King and that the bishop-elect should receive the temporalities of his see from the King and do homage for them. We do not know what was in the Emperor's mind when he saw his one-time worldly chaplain and favourite, now so completely changed, but we do know that he ran forward to embrace his young cousin, Count Godfrey, and treated him with such marked consideration and respect that the courtiers were amazed to see it. The two were received in public audience and were granted a charter approving the gift of Kappenberg and three adjoining estates to Norbert and taking the new foundation under imperial protection.

By the beginning of 1124 everything was settled and Count Godfrey, now free to enter religion, received the white habit from Norbert. From that day he would allow no allusion to his former rank and would accept no special treatment. He was genuinely upset if anyone addressed him as «Count» and insisted that he was the servant of them all. His life was one of extreme austerity and he gladly performed the most menial tasks. He had built a hostel for the poor, the sick and travellers outside the monastery gates and he would often go there and wait on the poor himself. In the following year, having completed his novitiate, he moved to Prémontré with Otto at the express wish of Norbert, who hoped that when his own strength should begin to fail and he could no longer carry on with his preaching journeys Godfrey might take over from him : but alas ! this was not to be. A year later Norbert, by now archbishop of Magdeburg, sent for him but Godfrey felt out of place in all the turmoil of an archbishop's court and asked permission to return to Ilbenstadt, where he went with Norbert's blessing. He was already in poor health and now his weakness increased daily so that he died at the age of thirty on 13 January, 1127, a few weeks after his arrival at Ilbenstadt. As he lay dying Otto and his brethren who were standing around his bed were weeping at the thought of losing him so soon, but he comforted them. Why else, he asked, did they willingly endure so many hardships in the religious life if it were not to find their happiness in Jesus Christ ? His shrine is still a place of pilgrimage and the feast of Saint Godfrey is celebrated each year on 16 January in the diocese of Mainz and the Order of Prémontré.

Jutta ended her days as Abbess of Herford whilst Otto became, in 1155, Provost of Kappenberg, where he died a saintly death on 27 January, 1172.

CHAPTER IX

THE APOSTLE OF ANTWERP.

Throughout the 12th Century, owing in large measure to the ignorance and lack of zeal of many priests, the worldliness of some bishops and the scandal created by the wealth of the Church, as well as to the injustices and violence all too prevalent in feudal society, there were sporadic outbreaks of heresy which took root and spread wherever conditions were favourable. So it was that about the year 1100 a preacher called Tanchelin or Tanchelm appeared in the province of Zeeland and began to spread his doctrines among the simple people of the islands and the coastal district between the Maas and the Scheldt. He rejected the authority of Pope, bishops and priests and claimed that he and his followers were the only true Church. He said that the sacraments were worse than useless, sources of defilement rather than of grace, since their efficacy depended entirely on the worthiness of their minister. In particular he preached vehemently against the Mass and the Holy Eucharist. He was a born leader as well as an eloquent and persuasive speaker, while his teaching had the appeal of novelty; but success came to him all the more easily because it was a long time since anyone had instructed his hearers in the truths of religion. He began by winning over the women and girls and then, through them, their fathers, husbands and brothers. At first he spoke surreptitiously to small groups but soon he was addressing large crowds in public places. He went about gaudily dressed in cloth of gold. Wherever he went he had a body-guard of armed men so that no bishop or lord dared to oppose him nor even to approach him. His enemies accused him of sexual promiscuity and of holding orgies but how much truth there may be in that we do not know.

Towards the year 1110 he extended his activities into Northern France and he seems at the same time to have changed his tactics for now, putting off his worldly finery, he began to dress as a monk so that he might be more acceptable as a holy man. About 1112 he went to Rome accompanied by an apostate priest who had espoused his cause but he met with no success there. On his return he was arrested in Cologne but soon managed to escape. In 1113 he was driven out of Bruges by the clergy and the people and in 1115 he was expelled from Louvain by the Duke of Lorraine. It was in this same year that he met his end for, as he was travelling along the Scheldt on a barge he was attacked by an infuriated priest and died of a fractured skull.

Tanchelin's heresy did not die with him and it remained particularly strong in Antwerp, which had become its principal stronghold. Antwerp was already a large and prosperous city, drawing its wealth from the trade which passed through its port, but its spiritual condition was truly deplorable.

The whole of the city was still one parish then and, although there was a fine large church, dedicated to Saint Michael, which had been made a collegiate church some time during the IIth century with an endowment for a provost and twelve canons, they confined themselves to carrying out the liturgical services in their church leaving the whole of the pastoral ministry to a single vicar. He was, not unnaturally, overwhelmed by the immensity of his task and seems to have lost any zeal that he might once have had; worse still, he seems to have become morally lax and had a good-looking young niece who was thought to be his mistress. It was not surprising, then, that his neglected flock fell an easy victim to Tanchelin and embraced his doctrines whole heartedly by the year 1108.

At this time Antwerp belonged to the diocese of Cambrai and the bishop was none other than Norbert's old friend, Burchard, who had been at court with him and had cared for him during his serious illness at Valenciennes in 1119. He must have heard of the success of his missionary preaching and the remarkable development of his Order and so it seemed to him that his best hope in this situation lay in enlisting the help of Norbert and some of his priests. Accordingly he readily approved of a generous suggestion of the Provost and Canons of Saint Michael's that their church should be offered to Norbert if he would agree to make a foundation in Antwerp. Reluctant as he normally was at this time to establish his monasteries in towns, this was an appeal that he felt that he could not reject when he saw the desperate need of so many souls, and he set out without delay with two of his earliest and most trusted disciples, Evermode and Waltmann, and twelve of his priests chosen for their zeal and learning. On his arrival he went out at once among the people, approaching them with love and compassion. «Brothers», he said to them, «have no fear. It was in good faith that you accepted false doctrines because you sincerely believed that they were true. If only someone had come and taught you the truth you would readily have welcomed it». Meanwhile his companions, animated by the same sympathy and understanding, set to work giving them the religious instruction and spiritual ministrations of which they had been so long deprived. Norbert's appeal, inspired by love and supported by reason, proved irresistible. He won over the minds and hearts of all so that they abjured their heresy and returned to the practice of their religion. Many of them, when they came to confession, brought consecrated hosts that they had been keeping hidden in boxes and odd corners of their houses for years. The outstanding importance of Norbert's achievement in Antwerp is shown by the fact that he is represented in art holding a monstrance in his hands. The Mass and the Blessed Sacrament were central to his spiritual life and his apostolate, and the rejection of them was fundamental to the heresy of Tanchelin.

Norbert settled his religious at Saint Michael's and appointed Waltmann as superior, whilst the provost and the secular canons moved to the Church of Our Lady, which was later to become the cathedral of Antwerp. At the same time they drew up and signed a formal deed of transfer, including in their donation not only the Church of Saint Michael but also the chapels in the cemetery as well as four of their twelve prebends. The White Canons were given the right to baptize at Easter and Whitsun, to visit the sick and give them the sacraments, to hear confessions and to bury the dead – in a word to exercise all the functions of parish clergy. Any gift of land or other property made by a parishioner during his last illness was to be divided equally between the two churches but a gift from an outsider or from a parishioner who was in full health was to be kept by the church to which it was made. There was to be a perpetual confraternity of prayer and mutual help between the two communities. Finally the whole transaction was ratified by a charter granted by the Bishop in this same year, 1124.

This is a convenient point at which to pause and review

the growth of the Order during the first few years of its existence. We have already mentioned Floreffe and the three German houses at Kappenberg, Varlar and Ilbenstadt but there were others. As early as 1121 the Lord of La Ferté-Milon had given the manor of Viviers, situated on the edge of the forest of Villers-Cotterêts, for a foundation and the Bishop of Soissons had given his approval in a charter dated in the same year, but it seems that some little time may have elapsed before Norbert took formal possession and installed his brethren, an occasion that was particularly memorable because of something that happened on the same day. It was very hot and a countryman who had been working in the fields all the morning was so thirsty by midday that he went to drink at a spring near by. When he bent down to do so he saw with a shock of horror a monstrous image reflected in the water. He looked up in terror and there was a tall figure all in black, who asked him whose man he was and promised to make him rich if he would become his servant. Thinking that it was a monk the man replied : «Keep what is yours. Our master is Norbert and he gives us all we need for body and soul». At this the demon became enraged and then disappeared, crying out : «Norbert ! Norbert !» as if in pain. Thereupon the man threw down his mattock and began to rush hither and thither, shouting like a madman. His neighbours, who were working close at hand, came running up and, seeing that he was out of his mind, caught hold of him, bound him and took him to the church at Viviers.

It was already evening when Norbert arrived with the Archdeacon of Soissons, in whose gift the church was. All the while the man had continued to suffer terribly and so the people brought him to Norbert and begged him to help. He made the sign of the cross and prayed over him, commending him especially to Our Lady to whom the church was dedicated, and soon he became quite calm and began to speak sensibly. When they saw this the onlookers were delighted and thanked God. «Now,» they said, «the good father who has just come here exhausted after his long journey can rest a little». «Not so», he replied, «the demon is only lying low. As soon as we go away it will torture him more cruelly than ever. There is some good reason why he was fallen into the power of this enemy. Let us leave him tonight and pray for him and tomorrow perhaps God will have pity on him». So it was that as soon as they left he began to shout and rage more furiously than before and the next morning, when Norbert came to him followed by many of the villagers who were curious to see what would happen, the man was completely cured and gave a lucid account of what had happened to him.

It was also in 1121 that a monastery was founded at Saint-Josse-au-Bois where a priest called Milo had come to live as a hermit beside a little chapel. Soon he had been joined by a number of men who wanted to live under his direction. Realizing the need for a definite rule he went to Prémontré, where Norbert was then building the monastery to ask for affiliation to his institute. Norbert agreed and went himself to visit the new community and encourage its members. It flourished greatly and within a year two daughter houses were founded from it whilst Milo eventually became a bishop.

Much more famous than these was the monastery founded by Luke, Rural Dean at Laon, who resigned his office to withdraw from the world in 1114. He settled in a remote place at the foot of the mountain of Cuissy, near the river Aisne, where there was a small chapel dedicated to Our Lady which the Bishop gave to him.

Here he was soon joined by others who shared his ideals and began to live a strict religious life as well as evangelizing the neighbouring parishes. In 1117 the Bishop confirmed the foundation by a charter securing them in their modest property and when Prémontré was founded he advised Luke to apply for affiliation to the new society. He went to Prémontré, where he was made most welcome by Norbert who willingly gave the white habit to him and his companions. This was in 1122 and two years later Bishop Bartholomew raised Cuissy to the status of an abbey and blessed Luke as abbot.

Meanwhile in the Collegiate Church of Saint Martin at Laon things had gone from bad to worse since Norbert's fruitless attempt to reform the canons in 1119. Their affairs had been mismanaged and the property was becoming more and more dilapidated, whilst their religious observance had so greatly deteriorated and their numbers had become so reduced that the bishop saw no alternative to their disbandment. In these circumstances he had recourse once again to his friend at Prémontré and asked him if he would take over the church. Norbert as we have already seen, was never keen on accepting a city church but, after some hesitation, he felt that in this case he could not refuse the bishop's request. Accordingly the latter granted a charter in 1124 in which he set forth his reasons for suppressing the chapter of secular canons and entrusted the church to Norbert in order that he might install a community of his canons following the Rule of Saint Augustine and the customs of Prémontré. (It is interesting that one of the witnesses whose seals were appended to the charter was Saint Bernard). Twelve canons were sent from Prémontré to inaugurate the new house and the first superior was Walter of Saint Maurice, one of the seven students who had joined Norbert from the School of Laon. At first the brethren had a hard struggle to survive. In the morning some of them would go out into the forest with a donkey, whom they called Burdin after the anti-pope, to cut wood which they sold in the town in order to buy bread and often there was nothing to eat in the house until they came back. The community worked hard, clearing the land, cultivating it and building their monastery, and their numbers increased so rapidly that in twelve years there were five hundred priests and brothers. Good administration and the generosity of benefactors made the abbey one of the richest in the diocese but its wealth was always used in the service of others. Not only were they generous in almsgiving but they also established a hostel which was always open to receive the poor and travellers. In due course Abbot Walter succeeded Bartholomew as Bishop of Laon.

Floreffe had already made two foundations – one for nuns near Cologne and the other for Canons in Liège where the bishop had offered them an oratory on Mont Cornillon in 1124. It was in this year also that monasteries were established in Lorraine and at Rieval in the Diocese of Toul and that Norbert himself founded a convent for nuns near Xanten.

At this time the White Canons only had diocesan approval from the bishops in whose dioceses the monasteries had been founded but in view of the rapid growth of their institute it had become necessary for them to obtain papal approval. Now in the summer of 1124 Norbert heard that the Cardinals Peter Pierleone and Gregory Papareschi, Legates of the Holy See, were holding their court at Noyon within a day's journey of Prémontré and so he went to present his petition to them. He was well received by the Legates who readily granted him a diploma of approval on 28 June 1124, in the following terms :

«We give thanks to Almighty God, whose mercy is to be preferred to all else in life, because he has inspired you to restore that excellent form of life of the holy fathers, founded on the teaching of the Apostles, which flourished in the early days of the Church but has almost died out since then» …

«The religious life is divided into two branches, sharing practically the same ideal, the canons and the monks. The latter, by God's mercy, has never ceased to shed its light throughout the whole world whilst the former, although it had well nigh disappeared with the decline of fervour in the Church, has experienced a marked renewal in our time. It was established by Urban, Pope and martyr; Augustine organized it by his Rule; Jerome reformed it by his letters. That is why it must be considered no less praiseworthy to revive this apostolic way of life, with the help of the Holy Spirit, than to maintain the monastic life in all its splendour by the grace of the same Spirit. Therefore, by the authority of the Holy See whose legates we are, we approve of your undertaking; we exhort and beg you in God's name to remain true to it».

It is worth noting the clear distinction made by the legates between monks and canons regular and their interest in the revival of the latter. This diploma set the seal of official recognition by the highest authority in the Church on the society that Norbert had founded and firmly established the Canons Regular of Prémontré as one of the religious orders of the Catholic Church.

CHAPTER X

COUNT THEOBALD'S AFFAIRS AND OTHER MATTERS.

The chronology of the life of Norbert between the beginning of 1123 and the end of 1125 is very uncertain and it is difficult to place events in their proper sequence. However it was probably no earlier than the summer of 1124 and perhaps even later (7) that Norbert was visited at Prémontré by one of the greatest nobles in France, Theobald IV, Count of Blois, the eldest son of Count Stephen of Blois and Adela, daughter of William the Conqueror. He had heard the story of Godfrey of Kappenberg and his brother, Otto; how they had given away all their possessions, changed their castles into monasteries and entered religion. He had been deeply moved by what he had heard and so now he had come to ask for spiritual guidance. When he met Norbert and listened to him he was so impressed by his attractive personality, his deep sincerity, his mature wisdom and the way in

(7) Abbot Madelaine quotes Abbot Hugo as dating the visit of Count Theobald no later than 1122 but this seems scarcely possible for it is inconceivable that Saint Norbert would have kept the Count waiting 3 or more years for the fulfillment of his promise to arrange a marriage for him. It seems more likely that it took place some time after Godfrey of Kappenberg had taken the habit early in 1124 and that when Saint Norbert made his promise to the Count he was already planning his journey to Rome to obtain papal approval of the Order, which suggests late 1124 or even 1125.

which he answered all his questions that he there and then offered himself and all his possessions unreservedly to Norbert just as Godfrey had done. Norbert, while fully aware of the good will and generosity that had inspired his offer, asked for a few days in which to think the matter over and seek God's guidance in prayer.

The position of Theobald was quite different from that of Godfrey, who could give his castle and manorial lands to the Church without causing any grave repercussions on society as a whole, but to understand what was involved in Theobald's offer we must glance briefly at the way in which France was governed at this time. Although the sovereignty of the King of France was universally recognized throughout the kingdom, it was only in the royal domain, comprising mainly the region round Paris and stretching as far South as Orleans and the Loire, that he ruled directly. His royal authority was sanctioned by tradition and the support of the Church, and hallowed by his coronation and anointing at Rheims, but his effective power came to him as ruler of the domain. The great vassals of the Crown such as the Dukes of Normandy, Britanny and Aquitaine and the Counts of Anjou, Blois, Champagne, Toulouse and so on, who ruled lands that might be as large or even larger than the royal domain, owed allegiance to the King, whose suzerainty they recognized, but in practice they acted as independent princes, entering into alliance with each other and fighting among themselves to maintain or enlarge their territories. The King himself was involved in these ever changing alliances and petty wars as he sought the support of one or other of his formidable vassals in his continual struggle to sustain and increase his authority. Moreover he and they alike had to be constantly prepared to wage war within their own dominions to maintain peace and order by subduing their unruly barons, who were in many cases no better than brigands. Theobald, who was surnamed «the Great», was one of the chief of these great vassals. He had succeeded to the county of Blois as an infant in 1102 when his father died in the Holy Land on the Crusades and his mother, a strong-minded princess and true daughter of William the Conqueror had ruled in his name for twenty years until she entered a convent and became a nun in 1122. His territory, which included the county of Chartres, bordered the royal domain and his power was greatly increased in 1125 when he inherited the county of Champagne from his cousin. Indeed his continental possessions were so important that, when the throne of England became vacant in 1135, he preferred to let his younger brother, Stephen, become King rather than leave France himself. Not only was Theobald active in the government and defence of his territories but he was also prominent in his day as a staunch supporter of the movement for reform in the Church. Norbert took all this into consideration and he realized that, if the Count's offer were accepted, it would result in the destruction of the whole framework of government in his dominions to the serious detriment of the kingdom as a whole and would bring ruin to many of his own people. Moreover Norbert had heard of all the good that the Count did – his great generosity in almsgiving, in building churches and monasteries and other religious and charitable foundations; he was always ready to help any good cause. It seemed to Norbert that Providence had placed Theobald where he could do the greatest good and that to change his state of life would be to go against the manifest will of God. Theobald came to see Norbert again a few days after their first talk, expecting that he would speak to him about the contempt that he should have for all worldly things and that he would urge him to renounce all his possessions and enter the religious life. Instead, to his surprise he told him that this was not to be but that his vocation was to continue to serve God in the world, as he had done hitherto, but with the added responsibilities of marriage so that he would have heirs to inherit his lands and carry on the traditions of his family, since it would be wrong to frustrate God's plans for him. Without any hesitation the Count accepted Norbert's decision and said that since this was the will of God he submitted himself to it but he insisted that, as it was Norbert who had told him that he must marry, it was he who must choose a wife for him. Reluctant though he was to involve himself in such matters Norbert felt that in the circumstances he had to accept this condition. He had already decided to go to Rome to ask the Pope for the final confirmation of his institute and so he said that he would take the Count's envoys with him. They could negotiate the marriage settlement and report back to the Count. He would so arrange his journey as to carry out his mission for the Count during the course of it. Nor did he leave Theobald without the spiritual direction that he had come to seek, explaining to him that, although he would live in the world and keep all his vast wealth and power, he could be poor in spirit and live as though he possessed nothing.

For the rest of his life Count Theobald was to live in close association with the Order of Prémontré. Wherever he went he always had two of the canons with him as his spiritual directors and agents in his works of charity. He also founded an abbey of White Canons beside his principal residence at Château-Thierry in 1133, although seven years later it was moved to Val Secret, a quieter and more secluded place.

There is an age-old tradition in the Order that it was

in Norbert's initiative in affiliating Count Theobald to Prémontré and in undertaking the direction of his spiritual life that the Norbertine Third Order had its origin. (8)

Norbert spent the winter of 1124 to 1125 at Prémontré and it happened that one night, when he was visiting the infirmary, he sat up late with the brothers there, talking and listening to what they had to say. As the night wore on some of them became very thirsty and he sent for water from the spring. No sooner had the brothers who had been sent to fetch it come into the room than Norbert asked why they were not bringing clean water. Quite taken aback they protested that the spring water was perfectly pure and the vessel in which they had brought it was spotless. They poured out two cupfuls but threw it away, Norbert firmly forbidding them to drink any of it. Then they took a light to examine the spring and found the body of an enormous toad putrefying there. (9)

According to both the early biographers at this time the brethren were sorely harassed by evil spirits, whilst the Devil appeared to Norbert, when he had been praying late at night in the church, in the form of a ferocious bear. After a moment of fright he saw through the illusion and with a prayer put the enemy to flight.

Perhaps the men of that period were too credulous about the activity of evil spirits in human affairs; perhaps we are too sceptical about the powers of evil. At all events Norbert was right when he told the brethren not to fear the Devil for he has no power to harm us except with our own consent.

(8) For the subject of the Norbertine Third Order see Appendix «B».
(9) Both Vita A and Vita B have a different – and less probable – version in which the toad is alive and crawling about on the bottom of the jug.

There are some stories about Norbert and the brethren at this time that remind one of the Little Flowers of Saint Francis. Thus one day some of the brothers who had gone out to cut wood came upon a wolf that was eating a kid. They chased him away and took the carcase back to the monastery where they hung it in the larder and thought no more of the matter. The wolf followed them and sat outside the door like a big dog, apparently begging for the return of his property. Some of the brethren found him there and tried to drive him away but he just looked up at them quietly and refused to move. When this was reported to Norbert he called the community together and said that there must be some reason why a fierce animal like a wolf should be so gentle in its behaviour. The brothers who had taken the kid now came forward and confessed what they had done. «Give back to him», Norbert said, «what belongs to him. You did wrong in taking what was not yours». When the carcass was given back to him the wolf went away peacefully doing no harm to anyone.

Another time one of the canons had been sent out to watch over the cattle in the fields but without a dog to help him. All day long a wolf remained with him, quite tame and apparently guarding the herd. Towards evening when it was time to take the cattle home, the wolf helped the brother to round them up and drive them back. When they were all in the enclosure the brother went into the monastery and shut the door, leaving the wolf outside. The wolf began pawing at the door and, as no one came, he kept on doing so to show that he wanted some one to come and give him a fair return for his day's work. It sounded as though there was someone knocking at the door and Norbert hearing it, asked why no one went to let the stranger in. When he was told that it was no stranger but a wolf that was making a nuisance of itself and refused to go away, he asked for an explanation but none of the brothers could give one until he sent for the brother who had been in charge of the cattle. He had been afraid to speak about what had happened but now, when he was asked who had been helping him with the cattle, he admitted that it was the wolf and told the story. When he heard this Norbert ordered that he should be given some food as a reward for his work. He seems to have become quite tame and soon he would even take bread from the hand of the boy who looked after the calves.

When Norbert first came to Prémontré there had been a hermit, called Guy, living in the valley and he had moved to the forest of Vicoigne, near Valenciennes. This forest had a bad reputation as the haunt of brigands so that no one travelled through it after dark or alone but only in well armed convoys. It was even rumoured that harmless hermits had been murdered there. However Guy was not in the least daunted and built a hut under an old lime tree close to a stream. Here he lived a life of prayer and preached to the people of the neighbourhood when they came to visit him. Soon he became a well known figure in the district, loved and venerated by all. Companions came to join him in his solitude and by 1125 they were so numerous that Guy had to consider the establishment of a regular monastery. Accordingly he applied to Gervase, Abbot of the Canons Regular of Arrouaise, who sent some of his priests to train the young community. They came but they did not like the conditions under which they were expected to live and left after a few days. Guy then remembered the saintly priest whom he had once met at Prémontré and decided to ask for affiliation to his Order. The canons of Vicoigne led a very austere life, working hard at clearing their land and making roads through the forest, which they freed from the brigands.

In this same year Norbert was approached by a certain man and his wife whose son had rejected them and given up his religion for the heresy of Tanchelin. The young man had been converted by Norbert and now in thanksgiving his parents offered some land for a monastery. This was colonised from Prémontré and was called the Abbey of Our Lady of Good Hope (Bonne Espérance). The young man entered the community at Prémontré where he died while still a deacon.

It was also in 1125 that King Louis VI of France, who had already confirmed Bishop Bartholomew's charter founding Prémontré, gave further proof of his esteem for the community by granting them some property near Laon which formed part of the royal domain.

The winter of 1124 to 1125 was one of appalling severity; there were exceptionally heavy falls of snow and the ice was thick enough in places to bear the weight of a heavily laden wagon. This was followed in the spring by storms which ruined the crops everywhere so that throughout the whole of France there was a famine which lasted until the harvest of 1126. Its consequences were aggravated by the plague which spread over all of Western Europe and in some places there were so many deaths that, in the words of the chronicler, «there were scarcely enough left alive to bury the bodies of the dead». In the face of this calamity it was the Church and in particular the monasteries that came to the aid of the people in their misery. Already when he was at Kappenberg in 1124 Norbert had foretold the famine in Westphalia and had said that the community would not escape it. All too soon his prediction was realized and the famine caused many deaths in the surrounding countryside. The community practised rigorous self-denial and never had their own meal until after they had seen their guests and the poor fed. One day, when Norbert was with them and the dinner bell went, there was not so much as a crust of bread left in the house. He told them to be of good heart and prayed with them; then, quite unexpectedly, provisions arrived, sent by some good friends in the neighbourhood. From that day they never lacked anything either for themselves or for those who depended on them.

The mother house of Prémontré adopted five hundred poor people whom they fed as long as the famine lasted and never bought food for the monastery without at the same time providing for the poor of the neighbourhood.

CHAPTER XI

PAPAL APPROVAL OF THE ORDER AND NORBERT'S FAREWELL TO PRÉMONTRÉ.

Norbert's success and the praise which his work won for him on all sides did not fail to arouse criticism and jealousy in certain quarters. Thus about 1125 Abbot Rupert of Deutz, who had already taken a dislike to Norbert when they met at Siegburg in 1115, attacked him in his book on the Rule of Saint Benedict. He accused him of adding unheard of austerities to the Rule of Saint Augustine, of never having a good word to say for the monks of Cluny and of claiming that monks were decadent and should be replaced by canons regular as being more perfect. «With all your virtues,» he wrote, «I wish that you had charity as well. Cease from persecuting me». Needless to say his accusations were quite groundless and there is no evidence of Norbert attacking either him or the Cluniac monks.

Another and more friendly critic, himself a canon regular, was full of praise for the White Canons' humble and austere lives as well as for their great hospitality but he was frankly shocked to see priests and even abbots engaged in such tasks as milking and cleaning out stables. Yet in this they were only recognizing the dignity of labour and, indeed, in these early days their poverty forced them to do the work of farm labourers.

The White Canons were also criticised for wearing woollen habits instead of linen tunics like other canons. It was contended that they were really monks and that they were presumptuous in claiming the right to be parish priests and missioners.

In the face of so much ill informed criticism and in view of the rapid and continuous growth of the Order, which after less than six years had nearly twenty monasteries, he decided to seek definitive approval by the Pope. Calixtus II, Norbert's patron, had died on 12 December 1124 and Lambert, Cardinal Bishop of Ostia, had been elected as his successor in the same month, taking the name of Honorius II. So during 1125 Norbert made preparations for his journey to Rome, the considerable expenses of which were borne by the monastery of Kappenberg. He set out towards the end of the year with Evermode, taking with him also Theobald's envoys since he was going to make a detour through Germany in order to arrange a marriage for the Count as he had promised. There was none of the pomp and magnificence that was customary for such an embassy. Norbert, in his old cassock and worn cloak rode a donkey and with Evermode observed as far as possible the same routine as in the monastery, faithful to the set hours of prayer and recollection.

They passed through Alsace, Würtemberg and Bavaria and so arrived at length at Regensburg. The Bishop at this time was Hartwic, brother of the Duke of Carinthia and also of Frederick, Archbishop of Cologne, who had ordained Norbert. He and Norbert had met at the court of the Emperor and they seem to have become friends. The Bishop had another brother, Englebert, Marquis of

Krayburg, one of the most powerful nobles in Germany, who had several daughters of marriageable age, and Norbert asked the hand of one of them, Mathilda by name, for Count Theobald. From all that he had heard about the Count the Marquis thought it a thoroughly suitable match and readily approved whilst Mathilda for her part gave her consent. So Norbert sent the envoys back to report to Theobald as soon as they had completed the formal marriage agreement.

As it was already late in the year and the weather was severe Norbert stayed for a short time at Regensburg but he gave himself no rest, going about the countryside preaching in the villages. Among his converts was an important nobleman, Count Albert of Pogen, who gave him his castle of Windberg to be a monastery.

Even the worst of the winter weather could not hold back Norbert beyond the beginning of January, when he went on his way with Evermode and two more of his canons who had joined him at Regensburg, so that it must have been about the middle of the month that they crossed the Alps, presumably by the Brenner Pass. As usual Norbert preached wherever they stopped and one of his sermons moved a certain count to found a monastery at Ursperg in the diocese of Augsburg «for brothers living according to the Rule of Saint Augustine and the constitutions of the venerable Norbert».

They arrived in Rome in the first half of February 1126 and Norbert lost no time in obtaining an audience with the Pope, who received him cordially. Having explained the history and nature of his Order and shown the letter of approval of the legates, he presented his petition for the solemn approbation of the Order by the Holy See.

Pope Honorius had no hesitation in granting his request and on 16 February 1126 issued a bull which began thus : –

«Honorius, Bishop, Servant of the Servants of God».
«To our beloved sons, Norbert, our brother in Christ, and the canons of the Church of Saint Mary at Prémontré, and their successors in the religious life for all time».

«Those who follow the way taught by the Apostles renounce worldly vanities and possessions and serve the Lord with all their might. If they persevere to the end in the good work that they have begun, they will receive the robe of immortality and everlasting glory at the last judgement. Since, therefore, inspired by the grace of God, you have resolved to live in religion and lead the canonical life, according to the precepts of the Blessed Augustine, we confirm your Institute by the authority of the Apostolic See and exhort you for the remission of your sins to remain steadfast in it. We command, therefore, that in the churches wherein your brothers live the canonical life it shall not be lawful for anyone to change the way of life established therein according to the Rule of Saint Augustine».

The bull proceeded to confirm the monasteries of the Order in their possessions and to take them under the protection of the Holy See, special mention being made of Saint Martin's at Laon, Viviers, Floreffe, Kappenberg, Varlar, Ilbenstadt and Saint Michael's in Antwerp.

Norbert spent some days in Rome as a pilgrim, visiting with his companions the tombs of the Apostles and the other shrines in the city, and at another audience he received a special bull for his beloved Kappenberg and also for Varlar and Ilbenstadt. It was dated 27 February and was addressed to «brother Norbert and his brethren living the religious life in the church of Saint Mary at Kappenberg». Finally on 4 March he was granted a bull in favour of Floreffe.

Having thus obtained all that he sought, he sent one

of his companions ahead of him to France by the most direct route to inform Count Theobald of his impending return so that he could let him know as soon as possible whether he agreed to the proposed marriage to Mathilda. Then he began the long journey home with the other two.

One night shortly before they left Rome, when he and his companions were meditating in church just before dawn, they all heard a voice announcing that Norbert would become Bishop of Parthenopolis during the year. They were deeply disturbed by this, Norbert most of all, but none of them dared to say a word about it to any of the others.

They crossed the Alps about the end of March and as they travelled through Germany Norbert preached to the people wherever they went. Near Memmingen, about 30 miles South of Ulm, he founded the monastery of Roth, which in due course was to be raised to the status of an imperial abbey and for several centuries exercised a far reaching influence for good.

Their route took them through Ulm and just before Easter, which fell on 11 April that year, they came to Würzburg, where the Bishop, who had been very popular, had recently died of the plague and the see was vacant. The clergy and the people insisted that Norbert should preside at the Holy Week ceremonies and so it happened that on Easter Sunday he was the celebrant at the High Mass in the cathedral. A blind woman, who was well known to everyone in the town, had taken her place near the sanctuary and immediately after the priest's communion she came forward and begged that she might see again. Touched by compassion Norbert, who had just received the Body and the Blood of Christ, breathed on her eyes and at once her sight was restored. Needless to say so public a miracle caused a sensation and everyone was eager to hear Norbert preach. Several of the most prominent citizens, all well to do, including a canon of the cathedral, offered themselves to serve God in the Order and so the monastery of Oberzell was founded a mile from the centre of the town.

Norbert was unhappy to find himself the object of so much praise and admiration, whilst his companions began to fear that he would be elected to the vacant bishopric. So without delay they slipped out of the town quietly in order that no one should notice their departure and continued their journey.

Their road home passed through Lorraine where Duke Simon, who had heard of their coming, gave Norbert a princely reception. The record of the ceremonies and the account of the expenditure on this occasion are still extant. The Duke was not disappointed in his guest; far from it, for he decided to found a monastery as a permanent memorial of the visit. As at Prémontré, Norbert chose a site that seemed to have little to commend it – in this case a fearsome solitude, about an hour's journey from the Duke's castle, where an unhealthy marsh lay in a gorge between jagged rocks, the haunt of wild beasts. The first community sent from Prémontré were frightened away but the superior appointed by Norbert had a stout heart and he brought in some religious from Rieval to replace them. This was Richard, one of the seven young Lorrainers who had joined Norbert from the school of Laon. He had given up riches and high rank in the world as well as a promising career to follow Christ in poverty and he proved an excellent choice, for the abbey of Sainte-Marie-au-Bois flourished under his rule. Later it was moved to Pont-à-Mousson, where it became famous as the centre of the reform in the 17th century.

Norbert reached Prémontré in May and, although his

early biographers tell us nothing about his homecoming, we can imagine with what joy he was welcomed by the community, how gladly they must have looked at the bull confirming the Order. They will also have heard with interest of his pilgrimage to the holy places in Rome and of all that happened on the long journey, particularly of the foundation of so many monasteries. Brother Godfrey of Kappenberg, who had just received the minor orders, and his brother, Otto, were now at Prémontré and it must have given them immense joy to see the bull giving special approval for the monasteries of Kappenberg, Varlar and Ilbenstadt.

Norbert's stay at Prémontré on this occasion was to be quite short – two months or even less – but he had a great deal to do to make sure that everything was in order for he seems to have known that his time was short.

Hitherto none of the superiors of the Order, except Luke at Cuissy whom Bishop Bartholomew had blessed as abbot in 1124, had been abbots, a title Norbert would never accept for himself, but now he arranged for Walter of Saint Martin's at Laon and Henry at Viviers to be blessed.

It was now that another monastery was added to the Order at Clairefontaine in the northern part of the diocese of Laon, where a certain Albert had recently founded a community on land given for that purpose by Guy, Lord of Guise. He has asked for affiliation to Prémontré but Norbert had not been able to undertake the responsibility at the time. Now, however, Albert had died and the members of the young community, having lost their founder, begged the bishop to intervene on their behalf. In the changed circumstances Norbert accepted their application and sent several canons from Prémontré to take charge with Gerard as their superior. He was another of the seven students of Laon who had joined Norbert, and

120

was the same Brother Gerard who had caused so much trouble and scandal in the early days, but had since then mended his ways and become a model religious.

It was in this same year that the canons regular of Steinfeld, near Cologne, who had come there nineteen years before from the abbey of Springiersbach, on the advice of Archbishop Frederick of Cologne sought and obtained affiliation to Prémontré.

The date was now drawing near on which Count Theobald's envoys had agreed that he should go to the appointed rendezvous to meet his bride and her father and he sent Norbert a pressing invitation to accompany him. This placed the latter in a quandary since, although it was he who had persuaded the Count to marry and had chosen his bride, yet he feared to go to Germany because of his premonition that he was to become a bishop there. In his perplexity he consulted a good friend, Geoffrey, Bishop of Chartres, relating to him how he had heard the voice foretelling that he would become a bishop that year but of what city or in what province he did not know. Because of this he was afraid to return to his native Germany, yet it seemed to him that he had a responsibility to the Count that he could not evade.

We do not know what advice the bishop gave him but probably the mere putting into words of his problem made it clear to him where his duty lay and that he must place all his trust in God's Providence.

We have already noticed the terrible famine of 1125 and have seen how five hundred of the poor were supported at Prémontré. Now on his return from Rome, when he examined the affairs of the community, he found that their lavish generosity in alsmgiving had imposed a severe strain on the resources of the house and he was angry at what seemed to him a lack of prudent management. On reflection, however, it appeared to him that he had been guilty of an offence against God and his brethren in finding fault with what was truly a work of charity to God's poor. He lost no time in publicly acknowledging his fault and making amends. He said that not only should the community continue to support the five hundred but that in his name a further one hundred and twenty should be added to their number. One hundred of these were to receive the same food as the canons, thirteen should be served with bread and meat and wine in the guest house whilst the remaining seven should take their meals with the community in the refectory.

This love of the poor was accompanied by a great love of poverty for Christ's sake and Norbert always liked to refer to Prémontré as «the house of our poverty».

Now the time had come when Norbert had to leave in order to joint Count Theobald at his residence of Château-Thierry and so, having made all the necessary arrangements for the good government of Prémontré and having given the community his final instruction on the religious life, its ideals and rewards and the dangers to be faced, he handed over to Hugh of Fosses and set out on his way.

It was with a very heavy heart that he said farewell to his brethren for he knew that he would never again return to live with them and, in the words of his earliest biographer, «like his Master, having loved his own he loved them to the end».

CHAPTER XII

THE RELUCTANT ARCHBISHOP.

In those days, out of reverence, even the most devout catholics only received communion three or four times a year, apart from occasions of special importance in their lives. Going to meet his future wife was such an occasion for Count Theobald and so Norbert, on his arrival, prepared him by hearing his confession and giving him Holy Communion. He also insisted that he should be reconciled to his neighbour and show compassion even to one who might be suffering through his own fault. There was a certain Humbert of Bar-sur-Aube who had been accused of some crime – what it was we do not know – and had tried to clear himself, according to the legal practice of the day, by the ordeal by combat. Being defeated he was considered guilty and sentenced to have his eyes put out and to forfeit all his goods. As a result his wife and children were starving and homeless, and he appealed for help to Norbert, who prevailed upon the Count to take pity and restore his property. It seems that the Count's officers were remiss in carrying out his orders for in the following year Saint Bernard and Geoffrey, Bishop of Chartres, reminded the Count of his promise to Norbert, and we must presume that he now honoured it for we hear no more of the matter.

Towards the end of June Count Theobald set out with a cortege consisting of his officials, representatives of the nobility and some of his close friends, whilst Norbert came with him, accompanied as usual by two of his canons.

When they came to the agreed meeting place on the border between France and Germany there was a most unpleasant contretemps for there was no sign of the bride or her father but instead his envoys appeared announcing that Mathilda had suddenly become seriously ill and had been unable to continue her journey. The Count and his advisers did not know what to think. Was it perhaps a diplomatic illness, a mere pretext to conceal a change of mind or had the Marquis never really intended to honour his contract ? The problem was what to do and all agreed that the best course would be to persuade Norbert to go to Regensburg and tactfully ascertain the true position. They begged him earnestly to undertake this mission and he consented, much as it went against the grain, for it seemed to him that it would be shameful to fail the Count by not seeing through to the end this marriage for which he had made himself responsible.

The Count gave him a sum of money for the journey, which he accepted but sent back to Prémontré for the poor. It was his invariable rule to take no money on his journeys but to trust in Providence and live on the charity of the faithful, like the Apostles when Our Lord sent them out.

His road took him through Speyer, where he had to cross the Rhine but when he reached that city he found it crowded with all the notables of Germany, ecclesiastical and lay, who had been summoned by the King to attend a diet, at which two cardinals were also to be present as papal legates.

The Emperor Henry V had died childless in May 1125 and with him the Salian house had come to an end after just a century. His nearest surviving relatives were his nephews, Frederick, Duke of Swabia, and Conrad, Duke of Franconia, the sons of his sister, Agnes, and if precedent had been followed, the electors would have chosen Frederick to succeed him as having the strongest hereditary claim. This had been the wish of Henry V and it probably would have been realized but for the determined opposition of Adalbert, Archbishop of Mainz, whose office gave him the initiative in the election. He was an ambitious man and there had been bitter enmity between him and Henry V, who had imprisoned him without trial from 1113 until forced to release him nearly three years later. Now his hostility to the family led him to press the candidature of Lothar, Duke of Saxony, who also won the support of the Archbishop of Cologne and the other bishops with the result that the rest of the electors came over to him and he was elected King of Germany on 30 August and crowned at Aachen on 13 September. He would not be Emperor, strictly speaking, until his coronation in Rome by the Pope, before which he would rule the empire with the title of King of the Romans.

Lothar III had risen to the throne of Germany from the ranks of the lesser nobility. As Count of Supplinburg he had advanced his fortunes by his marriage to Richenza, the heiress of the powerful Counts of Nordheim and Brunswick and, when the last of the ducal family of Billung died in 1106, Henry V appointed him Duke of Saxony. He «was a typical member of the Saxon nobility, a good soldier, conservative in his ideas, especially as duke, to maintain the aloofness and independence of his duchy. He was a solid man, who could be relied upon to uphold the dignity of the German Kingdom now that the independence of Saxony was not in question; he was also a scrupulous man of whom the Church need have no fear.

The ecclesiastical hierarchy had been largely responsible for his election; the Pope (Honorius II) through his legates had given it his blessing. As Duke of Saxony, too, he had been allied with the Pope against the king, and he justified the Church's confidence by making no attempt to claim for himself the rights at episcopal elections granted in the Concordat of Worms to his predecessor». (c) He always remained loyal to the Church and «was therefore constantly assured of the support of the Church in his German and in his Italian Kingdom». (c)

Conrad of Franconia was ambitious for the crown and lost no opportunity of stirring up civil war against Lothar. His brother, Frederick, on the other hand, had no such ambition, being satisfied with his duchy of Swabia in which he had consolidated his power and his only interest now lay in adding to it the family estates inherited from Henry V. During his last years the late Emperor had been acquiring lands for the royal domain and now Frederick claimed these as part of his inheritance. Lothar also laid claim to them as being royal and not personal property and a diet at Regensburg decided firmly in his favour. Frederick and Conrad refused to accept this ruling and, being placed under the ban of the Kingdom in January 1126, levied civil war.

The city of Speyer sided with the rebels against the King but, when he took it, he pardoned the inhabitants at the intercession of Archbishop Adalbert and summoned a diet of the kingdom to meet there in July.

When Norbert arrived, in addition to all the bishops and nobles and their retinues, there was present in the city a delegation from the cathedral chapter of Magdeburg and representatives of the citizens. Their archbishop had

(c) «A History of Europe from 911 to 1198» by Z.N. Brooke, p. 266.

died and the see had been vacant for some time. There had been three candidates of whom the most eligible seems to have been the subdeacon Conrad, son of the Count of Querfurt, who had received the unanimous suffrages of the clergy, the nobility and the burgesses and had been accepted for a time as archbishop elect. However Conrad, abbot of a monastery on the outskirts of Magdeburg, had opposed the election and won over the provost of the cathedral to support him in his contention that it was invalid on the ground that canon law did not allow a mere subdeacon to be raised to an archbishopric. This sparked off a controversy that apparently gave rise to irreconcilable differences among the electors. Lothar held his court at Magdeburg at Easter 1126 in the hope of finding a solution but without success, and so he referred the matter to the diet for a decision and summoned the representatives of the clergy and laity of the diocese to attend.

Norbert would have liked to pass through Speyer unnoticed but he was too well known and news of his arrival, spreading rapidly throughout the city, soon reached the court and the King himself. He received an invitation, which was more in the nature of a royal command, to preach the opening sermon of the diet in the cathedral and everyone who could do so came to hear him. His sermon was apt for the occasion – on the duties of christian rulers and their subjects, on the government of the Church and the election of bishops. He spoke with all his usual eloquence and persuasiveness, and his words had an immediate effect in promoting a sincere spirit of reconciliation between the King and the citizens of Speyer and in allaying the dissensions among the delegates from Magdeburg.

He was anxious to be on his way without any further

delay but the King insisted on keeping him a little longer so that he might have the benefit of his advice and three days later the affair of Magdeburg came before the council.

The representatives of the cathedral chapter put into effect a resolution that they had made earlier, to leave the choice of an archbishop to the Legates. It seems that they even offered a sum of money as a fee because the Legates indignantly rejected their request saying that where the Holy See was concerned there must not be even the slightest suspicion of simony.

So once again they proceeded to an election and this time also there were three candidates – Conrad of Querfurt, Adalbero, Dean of Metz, and Norbert, whose name had been put forward without his knowledge. The electors seemed to be quite unable to make up their minds which of the three to choose and Norbert, whose fears must have been increased by his awareness that the Latin name of the vacant see was Parthenopolis, the name he had heard in Rome, sat inconspicuously at the back of the hall hoping that no one would notice him. Then suddenly Adalbero stood up and pointed at him, saying that there was the man whom they should elect. Norbert would have escaped out of the hall and left the city at once, if he could, but, without giving him even a moment to collect his thoughts, the delegates from Magdeburg made for him and seized hold of him, shouting that it was he whom they elected as their father and bishop. Norbert was completely taken aback and protested strongly as they dragged him before the King and the Legates. The senior Legate, Cardinal Gerard, immediately rose to confirm the election. «And we», he said, «in the Name of the Father and of the Son and of the Holy Spirit elect and name as your bishop the Lord Norbert, a man of proved virtue. We are convinced that it was for this very purpose that God brought him here». Norbert pleaded his unworthiness and his complete inadequacy for such a responsible office but in vain. The King, after taking counsel with the Legate, the Archbishop of Mainz and Dean Adalbero, gave his approval and having received his homage invested him with the temporalities of the see. Then, like some sacrificial victim the archbishop elect was escorted to the cathedral where the pastoral staff was pressed into his unwilling hands by the Legate, who commanded him not to resist God's call.

Norbert was overwhelmed by the force of the arguments that were brought against him but, above all, he could not refuse to obey a command given in the name of the supreme authority in the Church. To others an archbishopric might seem a most desirable prize, offering power, wealth and position, but for him it was a tremendous responsibility which he had to accept albeit with a sad and sorrowful heart.

He wished to execute Count Theobald's commission before going to take possession of his see, but this was not allowed, and so he sent one of his religious in his place. All was well; the marriage was duly celebrated, and Theobald and Mathilda had five sons and five daughters.

A message was sent to Prémontré to give the community the news of the unwelcome honour that had been imposed on their superior and, having taken leave of the King and the Legates, Norbert set out accompanied by two bishops, Otto of Halberstadt and Ludolph of Brandenburg, as well as the delegation from Magdeburg which had been at the diet. They travelled northwards by long daily stages so as to arrive more quickly and reached their destination on 18 July. As soon as he came in sight of the city Norbert dismounted and took off his shoes so that he might walk into it barefoot. Such an act of penance and humility did not seem peculiar to the men of the 12th century as it would to us today. Otto of Bamberg had acted in exactly the same way when he took possession of his diocese in 1103.

An immense crowd came out in holiday mood to greet their new Archbishop, congratulating themselves that they had such a famous man, with the reputation of a saint, who would add to the prestige of their city, while the poor and infirm were happy to think that they had a Bishop who would have compassion on them in their sufferings. When the cortege arrived everyone was amazed for, instead of seeing a great prelate in magnificent robes riding a richly caparisoned horse, they saw a gaunt, emaciated figure walking barefoot, clothed in a worn habit of coarse material.

On their arrival they all went in procession to the cathedral and thence to the palace, where there was to be a reception in honour of the Archbishop Elect. The porter who opened the gate to let in the distinghuished guests, suddenly caught sight of a poorly dressed man among them whom he took for a beggar. He spoke angrily to him, saying : «All the rest of the poor came in long ago. You have no business pushing in like this and jostling all these noble lords». Those who were coming on behind saw what had happened and called out to him : «You miserable wretch, what do you think you are doing ? Don't you know that this is our Bishop and your master ?». The poor fellow was appalled and started running away to hide himself; but Norbert called him back and said with a smile : «Don't be afraid, brother. Don't run away. You see me as I really am – not like those who have brought me here to live in this grand palace».

CHAPTER XIII

THE DIOCESE
OF MAGDEBURG.

Magdeburg was already at this time an important city, situated as it was on the River Elbe, which formed the boundary between the old duchy of Saxony and the Eastern territory added to it in the 10th century. It owed the creation of its archbishopric to the Emperor Otto the Great and Pope John XIII, who set it up in 962, and it had the six suffragan bishoprics of Merseburg, Meissen, Zeitz, Havelberg, and Brandenburg, and of Posen (or Poznan) in Poland. It was given special privileges as a missionary archdiocese and had metropolitan jurisdiction over the area between the Rivers Elbe and Saale and the River Oder, covering most of the present day East Germany, as well as over all the peoples already converted in Poland as far as the Vistula. Indigenous to the area were the Slav tribes known as the Wends, who were largely heathen and unsubdued, although more than a century and a half had passed since Otto the Great had annexed the territory and instituted a policy which combined German colonization with the conversion of the Wends to Christanity.

One of the privileges of the archbishops of Magdeburg was that of being ordained by the Pope, if they were not already bishops, but it was decided with the legate's approval to forgo the privilege in Norbert's case in view of the length of time that the see had been vacant and the further delay that a journey to and from Rome would involve. Accordingly he was ordained in his own cathedral by one of his suffragans, Udo, Bishop of Zeitz, on 25 July, the Feast of Saint James. Nor did he go to Rome to receive the pallium, the symbol of metropolitan jurisdiction, which Pope Honorius, who had learnt of his election with the greatest pleasure, sent to him a few months later.

Never was there a bishop better fitted by nature, experience and grace to fill a see at a difficult time than Norbert proved himself to be at Magdeburg. He preached frequently to his people and instructed them but, above all, he taught them by the example of his own life. He banished all ostentation and luxury from his household and lived as simply and frugally as possible with the clergy of his court as though they were living in a monastery rather than a palace.

Once installed, he lost no time in examining the administration of his diocese, which had evidently been mismanaged for some time. He sent for those in charge of the various departments and ordered an investigation to ascertain the total income of the archbishopric, the sources of its revenue and who was responsible for collecting it. He also called for an estimate of all the expenses to be met out of the income. When every item was brought to account and a balance drawn up it was found that the income from all sources was barely sufficient to cover the expenses of the archbishop's household and the diocesan administration for four months out of the twelve. The Archbishop was amazed and instituted a thorough inquiry to discover whether the diocese had once been better endowed and its property squandered by careless administration. At last he learnt the truth, that originally it had been generously endowed by the Emperor Otto when he founded it and had later been enriched by further benefactions. When he asked what had happened to all this property and how so much of it had come to be alienated, he was told that some of his predecessors had given estates to members of their families or granted them as fiefs, whilst others had been negligent or too weak to defend church property when powerful lords had seized it forcibly. Thus through nepotism, violence and maladministration a wealthy diocese had become impoverished.

Although Norbert loved poverty and always lived as a poor man himself, he had taken a solemn oath, when he became a bishop, to defend the property of God's Church, which was also the patrimony of the poor, and so now he acted fearlessly. He sent out commissioners to every place in the diocese with an injunction that anyone who was in illegal possession of church property should refrain from acting as its owner unless he could establish a prior hereditary claim or prove that his family had held it from ancient times. The wrongful possessors of church property were highly indignant at the idea that a poor man with no armed force to back him, who had only recently come among them with no better mount than a donkey, should dare to issue such a stern and peremptory order. They ignored his demand, thinking that he was in no position to deprive them of what they had taken by force of arms or the threat of it. Seeing that they were recalcitrant, Norbert took a strong line and excommunicated them. This was an unpleasant surprise for them because the consequences of excommunication were serious in those days, entailing severe penalties in civil law; after a year they would be outlawed and lose the right to be heard in the courts of law. So most of them surrendered the estates that they held unlawfully but they did so with an ill will that gave rise to a smouldering fire of hatred and resentment which was later to break out into a fierce flame when the time and place should favour them.

Another matter that called for early attention was that of the discipline and morals of the clergy.

Norbert found that the law of celibacy was disregarded by many of his priests; some were living with women, whilst others had even contracted marriages in defiance of canon law and the repeated edicts of the popes. As recently as three years earlier, in 1123, the First Lateran Council had reiterated the law of clerical celibacy and had made the marriage of those in major orders not merely illicit but also invalid. Norbert's recent predecessors, pious and worthy though they might be in their personal lives, had left their clergy undisturbed to live as they chose but now he took a firm stand and issued instructions to the rural deans, the parish priests and all in major orders that they must observe the law in future and live continently under pain of forfeiting all ecclesiastical benefices otherwise. By this action he was laying up serious trouble, and even danger, for himself in the future. It was deeply resented by the clergy as an intolerable imposition that a stranger should come among them and interfere with their ancient customs and established way of life. So it was that among both the clergy and the laity there were many who felt that they had been sadly deceived as to the nature of the Archbishop whom they had elected and welcomed so enthusiastically. Where before no praise could be too high for him now he was the object of bitter hostility and vituperation.

In the 12th century, in addition to his pastoral responsibilities, a bishop had an important part to play in the civil administration. Moreover Otto the Great had delegated the royal authority over the cathedral cities and the surrounding country to the bishops of Germany, investing them with the powers of counts. The archbishops were among the King's principal advisers and frequently had to leave their dioceses in obedience to a royal summons to attend a diet or assist the King in important affairs of Church or State. The Church also exercised a powerful influence in mediaeval society towards mitigating the violence and injustice that were all too prevalent and towards ensuring that the savage justice of the day was tempered by mercy. Towards the end of 1126 the King and the Cardinal Legate, Gerard, called Norbert together with the archbishops of Mainz and Bremen to a meeting at Strasburg. It was apparently on his way back that he passed through Halberstadt, where there was trouble between the Bishop, Otto, and his clergy and people. Norbert and the Archbishop of Mainz had been entrusted by the King with the task of effecting a settlement, but they evidently were unsuccessful for a year later the case was referred to Rome with the result that the Bishop was convicted of simony and deposed by the Pope.

On 20 March 1127 Norbert ordained Meingot, who had been elected Bishop of Merseburg on 26 May the previous year. The delay of nearly ten months was due to the need for Norbert to receive the pallium before he could exercise his full powers as metropolitan.

Although the archbishopric of Magdeburg had been created as a missionary territory for the express purpose of converting the Wends, hardly anything had been done in this direction during the century and a half of its existence. Very few of the Wends had become christian and their pagan temples were to be found everywhere, their principal religious centre being the great temple at Rethra in the extreme North of the province. It was not to be expected that Norbert who, according to an ancient chronicler, had once dreamed of preaching the Gospel to the heathen and to whom Providence, it seemed, now offered a chance to realize his dream should allow any avoidable delay in putting his hand to the work. It looked as though his opportunity had come when King Lothar led an expedition into the land of the Wends early in 1127 and it may well be that he had already discussed the project with Norbert when he was at Strasburg at the end of the previous year.

For more than a century the German kings had shown little interest in this territory and had made no effort to consolidate their power and assimilate the Wends but Lothar III now resumed the old policy of the «Drang nach Osten» or thrust to the East. The expedition, which Norbert accompanied, started from Magdeburg and its first objective was Havelberg, where the Wendish prince, Witikind, who was a christian, submitted and promised to do his best to forward the conversion of his people. Thence they marched northwards and eventually came to Rethra, which they found deserted, the inhabitants having fled into the surrounding marshes. Everywhere they had gone the inhabitants had submitted but the expedition had no lasting results and later that same year the Wends celebrated the feast of their god, Gerovit, at Rethra with special solemnity. As for Norbert, he had achieved nothing, which is not altogether surprising since he could not speak the language of the Wends and they saw him only as a representative of the German invader and, therefore, as an enemy and oppressor of their people.

Later this year he was visited by Otto, the saintly Bishop of Bamberg, who was on his way to work as a missionary in Pomerania. He was a friend of Norbert and was received by him with great honour after which he went on through the diocese of Havelberg and a vast forest, which it took five days to traverse, until he came to a tribe of Wends who lived round Lake Muritz in the far North. They asked him to instruct them in the faith and baptize them but, when he referred them to their own Archbishop, Norbert, they protested that they could never endure his oppressive yoke. He left them after promising that, when he had completed his work among the Pomeranians, he would come back to them provided that the Pope gave his approval and their Archbishop agreed.

Although Norbert's many other duties never allowed him to work as a missionary himself, he is one of the saints who have been called apostles of the Slavs for he gave the initial impetus to the mission to the Wends and organised it by establishing his monasteries as missionary centres. Fifty years later his White Canons completed the conversion of the Wends and a German Protestant writer, M. Winter, has stated that this is the only instance in the Middle Ages of a whole nation being converted by a single religious order.

CHAPTER XIV

THE ORGANIZATION OF THE ORDER.

Even after he became archbishop Norbert remained a canon regular and a member of the Order which he had founded; faithful to his vows and to the Rule, he lived the same kind of life in his palace as he had lived in the monastery at Prémontré and he continued to wear his religious habit to the end of his life. (10)

All his efforts were directed towards spreading the spirit and ideals of the Gospel among his people and making them better christians but he was convinced that he could only succeed in this by giving them holy and zealous priests. To this end he introduced into his diocese the movement of reform which had been at work elsewhere in the Church since the middle of the previous century. His love for souls and his missionary zeal found an outlet in his pastoral visitations; there was no corner of his diocese, however remote, that he did not visit to preach to his people, to instruct them in their religion and to bring peace where there had been discord.

The monasteries and convents, being the principal centres of christian life, were the objects of his special care. He gave them every support and encouragement and

(10) It was not until later that the Church laid it down that canons regular who became bishops should dress like other bishops. Other regulars continued to wear robes in the colour of their order's habit until Pope Paul VI abolished this privilege and ordered that all bishops should be dressed alike.

watched over their interests but, where he found discipline relaxed or religious duties neglected, he took stern measures with any who refused to mend their ways. Where no religious houses existed he encouraged their foundation. In particular he was a frequent visitor to the Benedictine Abbey of Bergen on the outskirts of Magdeburg, where he went from time to time during the early years of his episcopate for a little peace and spiritual refreshment. He soon formed a friendship with the Abbot, whom he held in special esteem because of the high standard of discipline and observance that he maintained in his house.

The opposition to reform among both the clergy and the laity was so widespread and their hostility so bitter that, distasteful as he found it, he was forced to resort to censure and even excommunication in dealing with the worst cases and to prepare the castles belonging to the archbishopric as possible refuges in case his opponents should resort to armed force.

One example of the difficulties that faced him must suffice. It was reported to him that the Abbey of Our Lady on the Saale had been sacked and burned to the ground and the monks driven out. He went there and reconsecrated the abbey church, which had providentially escaped the fire. He called on the culprits to make restitution but they defied him, resisting all his efforts at persuasion and even proved obdurate when he excommunicated them. So he called on the citizens of Magdeburg for help and the castle of the offenders was captured and razed to the ground.

It was not only the administration of his diocese and his pastoral duties that occupied Norbert; considerable demands were made upon his time by the affairs of state. Thus at Christmas in 1127 he was at the royal court at

Würzburg together with the Archbishops of Mainz and Salzburg. Earlier in the month Conrad of Franconia, who was still in revolt and had recently met with some success in the field, had proclaimed himself King and, as soon as the news of this was received, the three archbishops excommunicated him.

In June 1128 Norbert was again at the court, this time at Aachen, and in the following month he revisited Xanten, at the invitation of his old friend, the Archbishop of Cologne, to consecrate the new collegiate church which replaced the old church so badly damaged by fire that it had to be completely rebuilt. The former canon of Xanten, who had been driven out by the enmity of his colleagues, was now a prince of the church whom they and the townspeople were proud to welcome back with every mark of honour. The celebrations lasted for two days; on 22 July the church itself, the high altar and the altar beneath the rood were consecrated and on the next day the side altars, the altar of Saint Peter behind the High Altar and the Lady Chapel. As a memento of this occasion he was given some relics of Saint Victor, the patron saint of Xanten, to whom he had a devotion.

For his first two years as Archbishop Norbert retained the office of superior at Prémontré and a continuous stream of visitors came from there and from other houses of the Order to consult him and to obtain his decision in matters of importance. It was, however, becoming increasingly clear that this could not continue indefinitely, for the Order needed a superior general who could devote the whole of his time and energy to its affairs. The news that came to Norbert from Prémontré and the other monasteries was most disturbing. Some of the religious were beginning to lose heart and to say, even to outsiders, that they would not be able to carry on any longer because the sheep will wander and become lost if the shepherd leaves the flock. There was a great deal of argument between those who insisted that they would have no superior except Norbert and those who had given up all hope of ever seeing him again and wished to elect another superior. Each side argued its case plausibly but neither could convince the other and the disagreement was having an unsettling effect on the young society. When he heard how things were Norbert began to fear that the Order so recently founded would wither and die if nothing was done to save it. Accordingly he summoned a conference of superiors and some of the senior and more prudent religious from Prémontré and other houses and asked what they thought should be done. He invited each of them to speak his mind freely and listened carefully to everything that was said so that he might give full weight to all their opinions and wishes in arriving at his final decision. There was considerable diversity in their views; some wished to join him at Magdeburg, whilst others wished to remain in their own monasteries but under his personal direction. Most of them, however, were for continuing to follow the Rule and the form of life instituted by him but under an elected superior and he was evidently of their mind.

As soon as the conference was over he sent them back to their monasteries except for a few whom he kept with him. His parting address to them was on his favourite theme, urging them insistently that they should live in perfect harmony, being of one mind and one heart, so that the peace of Christ and the love which He had taught by word and example might prevail amongst them.

Shortly after their departure Norbert sent several of his religious in whom he had special confidence to Prémontré to convey to the community his authority to elect a superior in his place and to inform them, without in any way seeking to impose his will on them, of this own preference as to his successor.

When in due course his envoys returned and told him that his own choice, Hugh of Fosses, had been unanimously elected, he was happy because he knew that Prémontré could not possibly be in better hands than those of his earliest companion whom he had trained in the religious life and who had been his right-hand man in the community. Yet he did not inform Hugh of his election for several days and ordered that it should be kept secret. This delay in confirming the election was in keeping with his invariable practice whenever he had to deal with any matter of unusual importance or was faced by a difficult problem. In such cases he would never make a hasty decision but would take time to seek God's will in prayer and get the best advice that he could by discussing the matter throughly with those around him. However, as it happened, Hugh already knew the result of the election for, as he afterwards revealed, very early on the day on which it was held he had a vision in which he found himself standing with Norbert in the presence of Christ. Our Lord stretched out His right hand in welcome when Norbert presented him with the words : «You entrusted him to me, Lord, and now I am returning him to Your Divine Majesty».

On the appointed day he assembled all the religious whom he had kept with him and announced his decision to them. Then he called Hugh to him and said : «It is you who have been elected by your brethren to succeed me in the house of our poverty». To this Hugh replied : «I must obey you and, above all I must obey God. I shall go forward trusting in His mercy. If He gives me success, thanks be to Him, but if not, then may I be allowed to return to you whom I have chosen as my spiriual father».

Whereupon Norbert blessed him, saying : «Go, for the hand of God will be with you to the end».

Having thus received the founder's blessing, Hugh left Magdeburg without delay, accompanied by Richard of Floreffe and Waltmann of Saint Michael's at Antwerp, and as soon as they reached home they were all blessed as abbots as also was Odo of Bonne Espérance. This was done on Norbert's express instructions for he had decided that the time had come for the houses of the Order to be ruled by abbots.

One of Hugh's first acts as abbot of Prémontré was to call a conference of abbots which was attended by these four as well as by the Abbots of Viviers and Saint Martin's at Laon, who had already received the abbatial blessing. The situation was one of such gravity that it did not permit of the delay that would have been involved in gathering a larger assembly, for the very survival of the Order was in question. Hitherto it had been held together by the personality of the founder but since his sudden departure from Prémontré it had been subject to such strains that in many places it had shown increasing signs of breaking up. Its growth had been so rapid that many of the brethren had little training or experience of the religious life and they came from a variety of backgrounds; the houses were widely dispersed and in many cases there was little contact between them; the Order had no organization and no constitutions to interpret the Rule and regulate daily life in the monasteries. Hugh was well aware of the dangers that threatened the very existence of the Order and saw clearly what must be done if it was to survive. He had been Norbert's confidant for eight years and no one knew the founder's mind better than he did; during Norbert's frequent absences it was he who had been left in charge at Prémontré and during his recent stay at Magdeburg they must have discussed the future of the Order so that we can be sure that what was agreed at this first meeting of abbots was in accordance with Norbert's clearly expressed views.

It was decided by the assembled abbots that the supreme authority and the final court of appeal in the Order should be a General Chapter on the Cistercian model to which all superiors, including the Abbot General, should be subject; the General Chapter should also be the legislative body which should make statutes to supplement the Rule, to define the duties of the religious (including all the officials) and to regulate the daily life in all the houses of the Order; the Abbot General and all the abbots and provosts should be elected for life; they should attend the General Chapter at Prémontré every year on the feast of Saint Denis (9 October).

As we have seen, there were only six abbots at this first meeting but there were nine in the second year, twelve in the third and eighteen in the fourth and the Order continued to grow so rapidly that by the end of Hugh's life in 1161 the number attending the General Chapter had risen to one hundred and twenty.

About the beginning of 1129 Norbert appointed and ordained a bishop for the diocese of Havelberg, which had been vacant since 1125. The long vacancy had been caused by the occupation of the town by the pagan Wends and even now it was not possible for the new Bishop to take possession of his see. His name was Anselm and he seems to have been a native of the Rhineland and to have studied at the school of Laon. At all events he was one of the early disciples of Norbert at Prémontré and had followed him to Magdeburg. He was to take a prominent part in public affairs and became a writer of some distinction. As Bishop he installed a cathedral chapter of White

Canons, with whom he lived in community, and he took an active part in the missionary work amongst the Wends.

One thing that Norbert had been determined to do ever since he came to Magdeburg was to bring his own White Canons into the diocese to help in the work of reform and in spreading the Gospel. He did not have to look far to find an opening, for opposite the Archbishop's palace there stood the Collegiate Church of Saint Mary which one of his predecessors had founded in 1015 and endowed for a dean and twelve secular canons. Now, just over a century later, their number seems to have risen to twenty but their condition had sadly deteriorated. The canons were lacking in zeal and far from edifying in the performance of their duties, whilst the buildings had fallen into disrepair and the church was roofless, little better than a ruin. Most of the church property had been shared out among themselves by the local gentry, some had been quietly appropriated by the neighbours (and there was no hope of recovering it), whilst most of what remained lay uncultivated through the negligence of the canons. As a result there was scarcely enough to provide a bare subsistence for the twelve canons whose duty it was to serve the church, and they were constantly complaining to the Archbishop about their plight. He was indeed moved by the sight of their destitution but, above all, he had the interests of his flock at heart and so he suggested that they should hand over their church to a community of canons regular and in return he would make a generous provision for them. He had already told the King what he proposed to do and had obtained his consent but, when he broached the subject to the canons of Saint Mary's they refused to consider his proposal and he met with equally strong opposition from the canons of the cathedral, who were the patrons of Saint Mary's. The

145

chapters of both churches were unanimous in asserting that it would be wrong to change the status of such an important church. They argued that what Norbert had in mind would be an infringement of the King's prerogatives since Saint Mary's was a royal foundation. They accused him of trying to intrude an alien community that would neither recognize the rights of the crown nor give the King the loyalty and obedience that were his due. They made representations to the King in this sense but without success since he had complete confidence in Norbert.

It was not Norbert's way to force his own will on others but he continued to press his case with the canons of the cathedral and those of Saint Mary's gently, patiently and persuasively so that, in the end, by dint of perseverance he won them over. The White Canons were established in Saint Mary's during the early part of 1129 and, as he had promised, he arranged that the secular canons should be as well, or even better, provided for than before, consulting their individual wishes as far as possible. Some were incorporated in other churches whilst others were given an income for life from the revenues of Saint Mary's. Norbert informed the Pope of what he had done, explaining his reasons, and obtained a bull confirming the new foundation. Saint Mary's at Magdeburg became the mother house of the Order in Saxony and was almost a second Prémontré until it was lost to the Order during the Protestant Reformation. Norbert entrusted to its care six of the city parishes and fourteen country churches and it sent out a stream of missionaries to work for the conversion of the Wends. For Norbert it became a spiritual home where he could retire from time to time to find among his own brethren a place for quiet recollection and refreshment of soul, and he remained its superior until the end of his life.

CHAPTER XV

THE UNPOPULAR REFORMER.

A reformer is seldom popular with those whom he sets out to reform and a reformer who is also a stranger, recently arrived, is likely to be doubly unpopular. The introduction of the White Canons into the diocese was the final act of provocation for Norbert's enemies, since in their eyes it was a reproach and a threat to their easy-going ways that would remain with them even after he had ceased to rule the diocese. It seemed to them that desperate measures were needed to remove their trouble-some Archbishop before it was too late and so now they began to plot against his life.

The first attempt was made on Maundy Thursday, which fell on 12 April in 1129. Norbert, who had been in attendance on the King at Goslar some sixty miles away as late as 10 april, had returned for the Holy Week services. Whilst he was sitting hearing confessions a young cleric, who was wearing a long cloak, came and asked the porter if he might go in to make his confession. When he was announced Norbert said that he was not to be admitted yet and so he was asked to wait. He became more and more impatient and kept demanding to be let in, but he had to wait until all the other penitents had been heard. When at last he was given permission to go in Norbert looked at him intently as he came through the door and ordered him to stand still and not to come any nearer. Then he called in the servants who were waiting outside and told them to remove the young man's cloak, which they did, revealing a sharp pointed knife about eighteen inches long hanging at his side. When Norbert began to question him, asking why he had come armed like that, he went down on his knees, trembling with fear, and confessed that he had been bribed to murder him. He was asked for the names of those involved in the plot and the bystanders heard with shocked amazement that the conspirators were to be found among the Archbishop's confidential advisers and others closely associated with him in the administration of the diocese, their leader being the Archdeacon, Hazeko. Norbert himself remained calm and cheerful, saying that it was fitting that this should have happened on the day on which Our Lord was betrayed and that he would have been happy to share in His Passion which had brought hope to the hopeless and pardon to sinners. The young man was imprisoned, not as a punishment but so that a full inquiry could be made into the details of the plot.

It was not long before another attempt was made on the Archbishop's life, this time by a cleric of his household who planned to kill him as he went into the cathedral for the night office. He hid behind a door, armed with a dagger, and waited until the Archbishop went past with his chaplains. It was dark and the clergy were all wearing hooded cloaks, but he knew that the Archbishop should be the last in the procession and so he stabbed the last one to go by but without killing his victim, who was saved by the thick folds of his cloak. The wounded man cried out and, when he heard the voice, he realized that he had made a mistake and took to his heels, shouting that he had struck the wrong man. (For some unknown reason the Archbishop was in the middle of the procession on this night). The others wanted to pursue the man and arrest him but Norbert told them to let him go, saying that one should not repay evil with evil; that the man had only been able to do what God permitted; that those who had sent him were determined not to rest until they had brought about his, Norbert's, death but that God's will would prevail in the end.

During the first half of June 1129 Norbert was again at Goslar for a diet of the kingdom but he was back at Magdeburg before the end of the month and now an event took place which brought the revolt of the malcontents to a head. It was reported to him confidentially that the Cathedral had been desecrated by the commission in it of some heinous crime, the nature of which has not come down to us. Norbert informed the Chapter immediately and said that in a case such as this canon law required a church to be reconsecrated. They disagreed saying that it was quite unacceptable that a consecration that had taken place in the presence of so many bishops and princes should be repeated. When Norbert found that nothing he could say would prevail against their opposition he told them that he would never celebrate Mass again in the Cathedral until it had been reconsecrated. It is difficult to understand the attitude of the Chapter and it has been suggested that their real motive lay in a quite groundless suspicion that Norbert intended under the pretext of consecrating the Cathedral to hand it over surreptitiously to his White Canons. Seeing that he had no hope of winning over the Chapter he explained the situation to the people in his sermon on 29 June, the Feast of Saints Peter and Paul, and told them what the law of the Church demanded in such cases.

That night he took with him two of his suffragan bishops who were in Magdeburg, Anselm of Havelberg and Godebold of Meissen, as well as Frederick, the Provost of the Cathedral, a few of the canons who had remained loyal and several of the religious of Saint Mary's, and secretly entered the church for the long ceremony of the consecration. About midnight, just as they had finished and before they had time to take off their vestments, they heard the sound of a large crowd approaching the Cathedral. The whole city was in an uproar because the Archbishop's enemies had sounded the alarm and spread a rumour that he had smashed the altars, rifled the shrines and reliquaries and broken into the treasury, and that he intended to abscond that very night under cover of darkness with all the relics and treasures belonging to the Cathedral. As they listened to the mob shouting threats and insults outside the locked doors even the bravest were frightened but Norbert wanted to go out and face the crowd. The others would not hear of this for, as they pointed out, no one would have the slightest chance of getting a hearing and pacifying such a riotous assembly, least of all in the dark, and they prevailed upon him to take refuge with them in a tower which stood adjacent to the Cathedral.

There they settled down to sit out the siege, still wearing their vestments, with little hope of escaping a violent death, and they could hear the crowd shouting to them to come out. Above this turmoil, in the top storey of the tower, Norbert and his companions sang the night office, while the clamour of the mob down below grew ever louder and more terrifying as they called for the Archbishop's death. The office that they were singing was that of the Commemoration of Saint Paul and some of them found encouragement in the readings which told the story of Saint Paul's sufferings and especially in his words : «I have not lost confidence, because I know who it is I have put my trust in». They took heart and were ready to face a martyr's death, if need be. Many of them, however, being weaker or less spiritual, were overcome by fear and complained bitterly. «Why», they said, «did we ever let ourselves be persuaded to follow this man ? Now we are going to die with him in our sins». Norbert did his best to encourage and comfort them. «Have courage», he said, «my dearest brothers, and do not be afraid. What we have done we did for God, what is happening to us now is by His permission. God sometimes allows those who do a good work for Him to be attacked by His enemies». He spoke to them again from time to time and continued to pray for them that they might not be overwhelmed by despair. As he said afterwards, it was not so much death that he feared as the danger of their giving way to despair. The weaker their spirits became, the more fervently he prayed for them.

Throughout all that night, whilst they were in these desperate straits, their adversaries were mustering their forces outside. At first light they launched their assault, some of them bringing up a battering ram, whilst others assailed the Archbishop and his companions with arrows and javelins, but a band of determined men, who had sworn to kill him, managed to get inside the tower and make their way to the top. As they were rushing in with drawn swords, Norbert came forward and stood in their path so as to save the others, and he said to them : «It is only one man that you are looking for. Here I am. Spare the others; they have done nothing to deserve death». The sudden appearance of the Archbishop in full pontificals and his commanding manner struck them with awe and they recoiled. His words went home and they fell on their knees, asking and receiving pardon, so that in a moment from being his enemies they became his defenders. Another group of attackers following them, came upon a knight of the Archbishop's household who was guarding a doorway. They were under the impression that Norbert had already been killed by the first group but were so incensed by the man's loyalty to his lord that they cut him down with a sword blow to the neck and left him for dead. Seeing this Norbert insisted, despite the efforts of the others to dissuade him, on running out into the crowd as though he were courting death, for he preferred to die himself rather than let anyone else die for him whilst he survived. Some of those in the crowd could not bring themselves to strike him, others aimed ineffectual blows, but the man who had wounded the knight, catching sight of him, advanced with the blood-stained sword in his hand and aimed a mighty blow at him. The sword struck him on the shoulder but seemed to rebound leaving him unharmed, although the pendants of the mitre were afterwards found to have been stained by blood from the sword.

Some of those who had instigated the riot but taken no active part in it, seeing that things had not turned out as they had hoped and that the Archbishop was still alive, hurriedly brought out some of the relics from the Cathedral, saying with a false pretence of sympathy what an abominable outrage it was that a bishop should be attacked like this by his own flock. They tried to take advantage of the situation to force him to agree to the expulsion of the White Canons from Saint Mary's but he flatly refused, saying that as long as he lived they would never succeed in undoing what had been done by royal authority and with papal approval, however little it might be to their liking.

At this point the city magistrate arrived and immediately set about restoring order. He had been out of town and had not known of the disturbance until the arrival of a messenger who had been sent hot-foot to summon him. He appointed a day on which he would hear any complaints against the Archbishop and would give judgement, whereupon they all dispersed in obedience to his order.

Norbert went into the Cathedral, which had been the source of all the trouble, to say a Mass of thanksgiving. When he had gone up to the altar, he turned and invited all those present to come forward and see for themselves that everything that he had been accused of stealing or breaking was safe and intact. Then he said Mass but he had to read the epistle and gospel himself because all the assistant clergy had gone to rest, utterly worn out by the fatigue and terrors of the past night. After Mass he walked briskly back to the palace with a light heart, thanking God for such a wonderful deliverance.

The malice of the Archbishop's enemies was only increased by the failure of their plot and they said that it was only by his magic arts that he had been able to trick them and escape death. They met in secret and agreed that they must at all costs rid themselves of this man who would never give up his efforts to reform them without any regard for their dignity and privileges or the standing of their city. They decided that on the day fixed for the magistrate's inquiry they would drink well so as to be in good form to press their case and if, as seemed likely, they could not win by legal means they would resort to violence and the Archbishop's death would be attributed to an accident during a drunken brawl rather than to premeditated murder. They decreed that if anyone should disobey them his house should be confiscated or demolished and all the contents appropriated by these self-appointed judges.

However the secret leaked out and word of the plot came to the ears of certain members of the nobility who were loyal to the Archbishop. They warned him of the danger and suggested that he should leave the city for the time being but he, rejoicing at the prospect of martyrdom, resisted all their efforts at persuasion.

On the day of the inquiry the conspirators gave the signal and soon the whole city was in a turmoil. When Norbert heard the uproar he asked what it was and was told that a large crowd had gathered outside Saint Mary's and was trying to drive out the brethren. He just smiled quietly and said that they could not succeed for the Heavenly Father would never allow what He had planted to be uprooted.

Meanwhile the rioting grew worse and, in the end, Norbert was force to yield to the insistence of those around him that he should leave the city and so, with a mounted escort, he went to the Abbey of Bergen in the suburbs. Not wishing to involve the monks in danger, he did not stay there long but, as soon as he had dealt with any urgent business and made the necessary arrangements for the administration of the diocese, he moved on to a castle belonging to the archbishopric, near Halle, hoping to find a quiet refuge there. However his enemies had forestalled him by occupying the castle of which they now closed the gates against him. In this extremity he turned for hospitality to a monastery of canons regular at a place called Neuwerk, which was not far away. Here he spent a few days in retreat, seeking God's guidance and praying for his estranged flock. From his place of refuge he appealed to them to be reconciled but, when they rejected his appeal and persisted in their rebellion, greatly as it grieved him, he had no alternative but to resort to excommunication. Meanwhile some of those who had remained loyal to him used their influence on his behalf and, by the grace of God, brought those who opposed him to a better frame of mind. They now came to him, repentant, acknowledging that they had been in the wrong and promising to make amends in whatever way he might decide. They also offered a large sum of money in compensation for the damage that they had done. He welcomed them with kindness but would not accept anything for himself; all that he wanted was to win their souls for God. He said that whatever he had suffered was on account of his own sins and that it was themselves that they hurt most by their offences. The only demand that he made of them was for adequate compensation for his knight who had been wounded and left half-dead. They were impressed by the way that he made light of the wrongs done to himself and was only concerned for the sufferings of one of his servants and were glad to be able to make peace with him by doing as he asked. They promised to rebuild the house of the knight, which had been destroyed, and gave him a sum of money in reparation for his wounding. Then they opened the gates of the castle, which they had till then kept closed against their Archbishop, and received him with every mark of honour. He returned home with a large escort of nobles, whilst the people thronged the streets to welcome him. They were full of enthusiasm and of admiration for the imperturbable courage which had brought him unscathed and confident through all his perils.

The sermon which Norbert preached to his people on his return has been preserved for us, the only one of which we have such a complete record. This is the substance of what he said : –

«With what grief I left you, my brothers, and with what immense joy, by God's mercy, I return to you. The enemy of souls establishes his empire by sowing hatred and strife, separating the shepherd from his flock so that he may bring the leaderless sheep into the abyss. The forces of evil were so powerful that my prayers proved of no avail and I was forced to fly. Now, Christ, who seemed to be asleep while the tempest raged, has spoken and there is perfect peace. I beg you, brothers, ardently to love this peace that God has restored to us, to seek it constantly and to cherish it carefully. Let our hearts be united in charity like those of the first Christians, of whom we read that «they had but one heart and one soul».

Do not be afraid, my dear children, that the wrong that you have done to your bishop may have turned him against you. Indeed it was not against the man that you committed your offence but against the priest. Nevertheless I am confident that, through the mercy of Him Who forgives us all our sins, your offence has been completely wiped out by your sincere contrition. Let us pray, therefore, to the Father of mercies and the God of all consolation that he may preserve for us this peace that He has given us, undeserving as we have been in the past, but which we must try to deserve in the future. Let us strive by good deeds to make up for the evil that we have done; let us stand firm in our vocation so that we may praise God together now and for ever. Amen».

Now that his position was at last secure Norbert could do something that the disturbances of recent months had prevented him from doing. His brethren, installed in Saint Mary's during the first half of 1129, had received papal approval on some date prior to 29 June but it was only now that he could issue the charter canonically confirming their foundation. Dated 29 October 1129, it set forth the reasons which had made it necessary to supersede the chapter of secular canons and the provision that had been made for them. It transferred all the property and rights belonging to Saint Mary's to the White Canons and, in order to ensure that they would remain at peace and unmolested, decreed that they should come under the immediate jurisdiction of the Archbishop and his successors.

Close to Saint Mary's there was a hospice, which had been founded by the first Archbishop of Magdeburg. Over the years its revenue had been misappropriated in favour of the well-to-do so that there was next to nothing left for the poor who should have received their daily sustenance at the hospice but now, in utter destitution, were reduced to begging. This was an abuse that Norbert, who was deeply touched by their misery, could not tolerate and so he spoke to the authorities and secured their consent for the transfer of the government of the hospice and all its property to the community of Saint Mary's who now assumed responsibility for its work. This took place in 1130 when the Archbishop issued a charter to ratify the transfer.

CHAPTER XVI

POPE AND ANTI-POPE.

Pope Honorius II died and was buried in the early hours of 14 February 1130. Then towards 9 o'clock those of the cardinals who were present elected one of their own number, Cardinal Gregory Papareschi, as Pope and he accepted, albeit with considerable reluctance, taking the name of Innocent II. Other cardinals, having heard what had happened, met about noon in Saint Mark's church and, disregarding the earlier election, voted for Cardinal Peter Pierleone, who chose to be known as Anacletus II.

The Schism which thus began arose out of the long-standing rivalry between the great Roman families of the Frangipani and the Pierleoni, who had been manoeuvering for power during the late Pope's illness. Innocent was supported by sixteen cardinals and, if he had been validly elected, then plainly any later election must be null and void. Anacletus did indeed claim that the first election had been uncanonical, having been carried out without waiting for all the cardinals to assemble, and that a majority, twenty seven as against sixteen, had voted for him. He succeeded in winning the support of most of the Roman clergy as well as of the nobility and people of Rome and occupied the principal churches and strong points in the City. Innocent was forced to leave and departed by sea, first for Pisa, where he stayed for several weeks, and then for France.

So far all the advantages seemed to rest with Anacletus but it remained to be seen which of the claimants would be recognized by the Church at large and each sent envoys and letters to the christian princes to notify them of his election and to seek their support. In France the King and the bishops declared for Innocent, largely through the influence of Saint Bernard, who also won over Henry I of England. However both of the claimants realized the importance of winning the recognition and support of Lothar, as ruler of the Empire and King of Italy. Accordingly they lost no time in writing to inform him of their election and each continued persistently to press his claim. However Lothar firmly refused to make any decision until he had referred the matter to a diet of the kingdom.

Bernard had decided for Innocent largely on moral grounds, because he considered him much worthier to be Pope than his rival. Indeed it was true that, whereas Innocent's character was above reproach, Anacletus had a bad reputation as being of doubtful morals, ambitious, grasping and corrupt. He owed his advancement to the influence of his family and there was more than a suspicion of simony about it.

Norbert, who by this time was one of Lothar's most trusted advisers, had met both Innocent and Anacletus for they had been the two Legates who gave papal approval to his Order in 1124, but he wanted to have all the facts about the double election before making up his mind. He wrote, therefore, to two of the Italian bishops, the Archbishop of Ravenna and the Bishop of Lucca, who would be in a better position than he was to know what had happened. In their letters they gave Norbert a detailed account of events and assured him that Innocent had been validly elected whereupon Peter Pierleone, who had long been plotting to become Pope, had summoned his own supporters among the cardinals and had been elected by them. He had then by violence and bribery gained control of Rome but he was nowhere accepted in Italy North of the City. (11)

These letters finally convinced Norbert beyond all doubt that Innocent was the lawful Pope and he spared no effort to secure his acceptance by Lothar and throughout Germany. At the diet which was held at Würzburg in October 1130 his powerful advocacy helped greatly to carry the day and now at last Lothar gave his decision in favour of Innocent. The diet declared Anacletus excommunicate and renewed the ban against Frederick of Swabia and Conrad of Franconia, and a deputation was sent under the leadership of the Archbishop of Salzburg and the Bishop of Münster to convey its decision in his favour to Innocent.

The Pope, who wished to meet Lothar, invited him to be present at a council which was to be held on the territory of the Empire at Liège early in the next year. The King accepted and came with his Queen and many of the bishops, abbots and chief nobles of Germany. When the Pope arrived for the opening ceremony on 22 March 1131 he was received by the King who held the stirrup for him to mount and led him through the streets, holding the bridle of his horse. In the council the Pope excommunicated the rebels, Frederick and Conrad, whilst the King promised to lead an expedition to depose the anti-pope. However Lothar could not resist the temptation to take advantage of the Pope's situation and, in

(11) Peter Pierleone, anticipating the Pope's death, had appeared before the papal palace at the head of a large crowd intending to claim that he had been elected by acclamation but his attempt was foiled because the Pope, who was still alive, showed himself at the window.

return for his support, he asked to be given back the rights of investiture of bishops. The Pope was taken aback by this request and seemed to hesitate but fortunately Bernard of Clairvaux spoke out strongly against conceding this claim and no more was heard of the matter on this occasion.

When the council was over the Pope went to Laon, where he celebrated mass in the Cathedral on Palm Sunday, 12 April, and in the White Canon's abbey church of Saint Martin on the Tuesday in Holy Week. Evidently Norbert assisted at the council and on 2 April he received a charter from the Pope confirming the foundation of Saint Mary's at Magdeburg. It would be pleasant to think that he accompanied the Pope to Laon and was able to visit Prémontré but this does not appear to have been the case for a serious situation had arisen at Magdeburg which required his immediate return. He must, however, have spoken to Innocent about Prémontré and the Order while he was at the council for, when Abbot Hugh was received in audience at Laon on 12 April and was given a bull taking the Order under the special protection of the Holy See and confirming its Rule and observances, the Pope particularly mentioned that it had been granted on Norbert's «just representations and at his request».

The trouble at Magdeburg had been stirred up by a faction in the Cathedral Chapter, led by Archdeacon Hazeko, which had never become truly reconciled to the Archbishop after the settlement following the disturbances in 1129. For reasons unknown to us – perhaps his persistent disloyalty, perhaps irregularities in the administration of church property, possibly for both reasons – Norbert found himself obliged to reprimand Hazeko in a chapter meeting and to suspend him from his functions, whereupon he promptly appealed to the Pope, as indeed several other members of the chapter had done. Norbert had done his best to avoid this situation for he found the appeals vexatious, being obstacles to the reforms that he was trying to introduce in his diocese.

Before the case could be decided Honorius II died and the ensuing schism seemed most opportune for Hazeko. Seeing that Norbert had recognized Innocent, he went over to the party of Anacletus and made his way to Rome to present his appeal in person. Anacletus welcomed him and sent him back with a letter dated 18 May 1130 in which he commanded Norbert to reinstate him and to come to Rome himself to receive judgement during the octave of Saint Martin, that is between 11 and 18 November. He also forbade him to hinder any of his canons who might wish to come to Rome. However, since he still had some hope of winning over Norbert, he ended on a conciliatory note, saying that it was not his desire to cause any offence but rather to prove his deep love and to honour him and his diocese.

When Hazeko presented this letter to the Archbishop on his return any hopes that he may have entertained were speedily dispelled since Norbert, regarding Anacletus as a rebel, paid no attention to his demands. Towards the end of the year Hazeko was back in Rome and was given another letter to deliver, extremely bitter in tone, accusing Norbert of spreading malicious falsehoods about Anacletus, of leading King Lothar astray and of suborning the loyalty of the bishops and nobles of Germany as well as of base ingratitude to a friend who, as legate in France, had given papal approval to his Order. It purported to excommunicate Norbert for his refusal to come to Rome for judgement in November. It was evidently the arrival of Hazeko with this letter which caused Norbert's hasty return from Liège.

In October 1131 there was an important council at Rheims, attended by some three hundred bishops from France, Germany, England and Spain. In addition to their main business, which was to confirm their recognition of Innocent and renew the sentence of excommunication against Anacletus, the bishops passed decrees against various abuses which required reform. King Louis of France came to Rheims on 24 October with his ten year old son whom he had crowned in the Cathedral on the next day. On 26 October Norbert arrived as Lothar's ambassador, accompanied by the Bishop of Hildesheim; he was received with all due honour and gave the Pope a letter in which the King announced his firm intention of leading an expedition to Rome to depose Anacletus.

Norbert had taken the opportunity to bring with him the ancient title deeds of his archdiocese, which had become so dilapidated and worm-eaten as to be practically illegible, and also other documents that he had recovered concerning the church property which had been misappropriated. He had them renewed and corrected and obtained papal confirmation of all the rights and privileges of the diocese of Magdeburg. He also received a secret authorisation to replace his cathedral chapter at an opportune moment by a community of his own White Canons, but he was never to have the time to do this.

The last act of the council was the canonisation of Godehard, a former Bishop of Hildesheim. The cause was promoted by his successor, Bishop Bernard, and was supported by Norbert acting on behalf of the King and the decree was promulgated on 29 October.

It was at this council that Norbert met his friend, Bishop Bartholomew for the last time. He also met the Bishop of Verdun, who asked him for some of his religious to take over the Abbey of Saint Paul at Verdun, which was heavily in debt and had become notorious for the scandalous life of its monks. Norbert agreed and arranged for a community to be sent from Prémontré.

This council at Rheims must have brought back to Norbert vivid memories of the earlier council which had been held in the same city exactly ten years before, of his meeting then with Bishop Bartholomew and of how he had been led to found Prémontré. One would dearly like to know whether he now went from Rheims to revisit Laon and Prémontré. Abbot Hugo thought that he did and may well have been right but alas ! there is no evidence of such a visit.

It was clear by now that Innocent was recognized as the lawful Pope by good catholics everywhere, although he was reduced to wandering about from place to place, whilst the intruder, Anacletus, supported by his family and friends and by Roger, the Norman ruler of Sicily, whom he had bribed with the title of King, remained master of Rome. It was plainly urgent that strong action should be taken to end the schism.

By the end of the year 1131 Norbert had founded two houses for his Order in the diocese of Magdeburg. The first was at Pölde, where there was a Benedictine monastery under the immediate jurisdiction of the Archbishop. A serious relaxation of discipline had set in about the year 1100 and the buildings had been allowed to become dilapidated. Norbert did all within his power to bring about a reform but all his remonstrances, and even censures, had no effect and there was no alternative but to expel the monks and replace them by another community. This he did, introducing canons regular of his own Order and appointing a priest from Magdeburg as provost, so that once again the monastery began to flourish materially and spiritually.

The story of the other foundation is given in considerable detail in the contemporary chronicle of Gottesgnaden. There was at that time a wealthy Saxon nobleman, Count Otto of Reveningen, who was highly respected by all and played a prominent part in public life. Although he had reached mature years, he was unmarried and there was no heir to his large estates. When Norbert came to know him it seemed to him that the Count might be destined to serve God and the Church in a very special manner and so he suggested to him that, since he had no relations to inherit his property, he might do well to make the Church of Christ his heir. From time to time, when they met, they spoke about this and finally Norbert's words proved so effective that the Count came and placed all that he possessed at his disposal. Together they formed a plan to build a church and monastery on one of the Count's estates and Norbert promised that it should always enjoy his special care and protection. A pleasant situation was chosen within easy reach of Magdeburg and work was begun on the buildings in 1131. The church was dedicated to Our Lady and Saint Victor and Norbert gave it the relics of that Saint which he had brought from Xanten. He also contributed generously to its endowment, whilst Count Otto gave it all his property except the castle of Reveningen, which he retained for the time being until he could be sure that the Archbishop's hopes for the new foundation would be realized. In the end he entered religion and was professed for the monastery which he had founded.

Norbert took no credit to himself for his part in the foundation and, apparently as the result of a vision, called the new house after the Grace of God, Gottesgnaden or Grâce Dieu. The first superior was Emelrich, whom Norbert had brought with him from France, but it was not long before he got permission to leave for the Holy Land, where he became a bishop. Evermode was then put in charge, not as provost but as administrator, for Norbert himself retained the office of superior until the end of his life.

Gottesgnaden, like Saint Mary's at Magdeburg, followed the Rule and usages of Prémontré with some slight differences. Thus Norbert gave permission for both communities to wear linen surplices as their daily dress and to have black cloaks. He also sanctioned the adoption of the breviary and chant in use in the cathedral of Magdeburg, which were the same as those of the secular clergy, which he had used himself when he was at Xanten.

During the years 1126 to 1131, in the midst of his tribulations, Norbert had the consolation of receiving news of the spread of his Order in various countries. While most of the foundations made at this time are no more than names to us, there are three in Belgium which still exist and play an important part in the life of the Church today.

The first is Grimbergen, which was founded for Augustinian canons in 1110, but they left after a few years and were replaced by Benedictine monks, who in their turn were forced out by their poverty and the attacks of certain malefactors. In this predicament a message was sent to Norbert at Magdeburg, appealing to him to take over the monastery. This he agreed to do after some hesitation and a colony from Prémontré made the new foundation in 1128.

The second is the abbey of Park, which was founded in 1129 by Godfrey, Duke of Lower Lorraine, for canons from Saint Martin's at Laon. Of special interest, however, to British and Irish readers is Tongerlo which is one of the largest Norbertine abbeys in the world, although its origin was quite humble since it was founded in 1130 not by a great noble but by a simple peasant farmer who became a laybrother in the abbey. Tongerlo is the mother house from which the abbey of Kilnacrott in Ireland and the priory of Storrington in England were founded.

The Abbey of Berne in the Netherlands was founded in 1134, the year of Norbert's death and as the mother house of the Abbey of De Pere it established the Order in the United States. It has also introduced the Order into India where it is already flourishing.

CHAPTER XVII

THE LAST JOURNEY.

On his return from Rheims Norbert presented the Pope's letter to the King, who had indeed already made up his mind to lead an army to Rome as soon as possible. To depose Anacletus and enthrone Innocent were not the only objects of his campaign since the Pope had promised to crown him in Rome as Emperor, which would greatly strengthen his position. He announced his intention at a diet held at Easter, appointed his son-in-law, Duke Henry of Bavaria, to administer the kingdom in his absence, and named Würzburg as the place where the army was to assemble on 15 August, the feast of the Assumption. Many of the German bishops were eager to go with the expedition but Norbert was anxious to return to his diocese where he still had a great deal to do. Moreover he was in poor health and physically exhausted, although he was as vigorous as ever in mind an spirit. However Lothar had come to depend on Norbert for whom he had a great affection and whose advice he followed mostly in affairs of state. So now he called on Norbert to accompany him, whilst the Pope commanded him under obedience to come. Events were to prove the immense value of his presence for the success of the expedition and the good of the Church.

Unfortunately it was necessary to leave enough troops in Germany to deal with the continuing rebellion of Fred-

erick of Swabia and so the force that gathered at Würzburg was much smaller than the armies which usually
went with the German Kings into Italy, the number being
only about 1500.

They reached Augsburg in the evening of 25 August
and, before going to pray in the cathedral, Norbert warned his deacon to take special care of the pallium and the
other articles for which he was responsible, as the city
was on the verge of insurrection and, sure enough, on
the following day the citizens launched an armed attack
on the soldiers. Lothar quickly rallied his troops and coun-
terattacked but in less than two hours most of this
prosperous city was a blaze. The Bishop of Augsburg,
who had been driven from his house and lost all his
possessions, was rescued by Norbert who found him
sitting alone in the main square and took him into his
own lodgings. Being at Augsburg, Norbert seized the
opportunity of visiting the abbey of his Order which had
been founded nearby at Ursperg seven years before.

The army resumed its march without delay and on 31
August entered Italy by the Brenner Pass and the valley
of the Trentino, the route always followed by German
armies in the Middle Ages. Conrad of Franconia, who
was in Lombardy and had recently had himself crowned
at Milan as King of Italy, was told that Lothar was approaching at the head of a large army. Believing this
rumour and being deserted by most of his followers he
fled back to Germany, leaving the road into Italy clear,
but Lothar had to advance through Lombardy with cau-
tion because his army was not strong enough to subdue
the more important towns such as Milan and Verona.

By ancient custom the Archbishop of Cologne was
Chancellor for Italy but Frederick of Carinthia had died
and his successor, Bruno, had not yet been ordained bish-

op. Accordingly Lothar appointed Norbert to take his place as Chancellor during this expedition.

The first meeting of the Pope and the King took place in the plain of Roncaglia, between Piacenza and Cremona, where they held a conference to decide on their plan of action. Thence they advanced into the territory of Bologna, which refused to open its gates to Lothar, and after Christmas they moved on separately, the Pope going through Pisa and along the coastal road, whilst the King marched down the centre of the peninsula. In March the Pope was at Viterbo and Lothar not very far away, at Valentano on the shore of Lake Bolsena. It was here that the envoys of Anacletus found the King and tried to win him over, using every possible argument in support of their case, but without success thanks to Norbert's powerful opposition. Then Anacletus devised a clever stratagem; he instructed his envoys to seek an audience with the King and to propose that he should set up an independent tribunal to judge between the claimants. This seemed so fair and reasonable that it attracted a great deal of support among those around Lothar as well as in the rest of the army.

Norbert, seeing the turn that events were taking, went without a moment's delay to the Pope at Viterbo and gave him a full account of what was happening in the royal camp. He warned him that in his own interests and those of the Church he must act promptly and take up the challenge. This advice was considered completely unacceptable by all the Pope's advisers, who argued that it was unthinkable that he should submit to any human authority or be judged by any tribunal. Innocent did not allow himself to be influenced by their opinion but made up his own mind. He agreed to the proposal and undertook to submit to life imprisonment if he should fail to appear at the appointed time and place. Thus the crafty plan of Anacletus, who had been counting on his refusal so as to discredit him in the eyes of the King, was foiled.

In April Lothar was on his way once more but, not being strong enough to advance directly on the City, he made a detour and approached Rome from the South. He first encamped on a hill outside the walls but on 30 April, entering the City by a bold move, he established himself on the Aventine, near Santa Sabina, and installed Innocent in the Lateran Palace.

Anacletus, safe in the castle of Sant Angelo, played for time, sending envoys to keep alive negotiations with Lothar but always evading any firm commitment. The King was loath to break off relations with him completely because he was in possession of Saint Peter's where the emperors were always crowned, and the royal army was not strong enough to occupy it by force. The Pope, for his part, was reluctant to crown Lothar before he had fulfilled his promise to depose Anacletus. It was through Norbert's tactful mediation that a solution was found and that it was arranged that Lothar should be crowned in the Lateran Basilica, which was, in fact, and still is the Pope's cathedral.

When the day came for the coronation all Rome was suddenly in a turmoil and the streets were full of rioting crowds, for the people feared that the crowning of Lothar by Innocent presaged the downfall of Anacletus. Nor were they far wrong for from that day Innocent gained ground continually at the expense of his rival.

At the appointed time Lothar, escorted by his troops, came to the Basilica where he was received by the Pope, with the cardinals, the bishops and the rest of the clergy in attendance. Amid the enthusiastic applause of the whole congregation Innocent placed the imperial crown of Charlemagne on his head and then crowned Queen Richenza as Empress.

At the banquet which followed the ceremony a deplorable quarrel broke out between the servants of the Abbot of Fulda and those of the Archbishop of Magdeburg as to which should take precedence. It was only the Abbot's timely arrival that prevented bloodshed. The dispute was referred to the Emperror who, in spite of Norbert's objection, decided in favour of the Abbot. This we learn from the chronicle of the Abbey of Fulda.

After the coronation the Emperor, somewhat unexpectedly, once again asked to be granted the right of investiture of bishops on the ground that it would strengthen the imperial authority and further cement the close relations existing between the Pope and the Emperor. Innocent did not appear to realize the danger that this would pose to the freedom of the Church under a ruler less well disposed than Lothar and seemed to be on the point of giving his consent. Not one of all the other bishops present protested; only Norbert came forward and spoke out boldly in front of the Emperor. «What are you doing, Holy Father ?», he said, «To whom are you going to hand over the flock entrusted to your care ? You have received the Church free, are you going to reduce her to slavery again ? The successor of Peter must act like Peter. I promised in the name of Christ to obey you but, if you do what is being asked of you, then I shall oppose you before the whole Church». The crisis passed and thanks to Norbert's skilful diplomacy, a satisfactory agreement was reached between the Pope and the Emperor. Then on June 8 Innocent granted Lothar, and his son-in-law, Duke Henry, after him, the life rent of the estates that the Countess Mathilda had left to the Church.

On the very day of the coronation the Pope issued a

bull in which he expressed his gratitude to Norbert and his appreciation of his services to the Holy See. It began thus : – «The Holy Roman and Apostolic Church, ever since it adopted you in a special manner as its son, has given sure tokens of its recognition of the zeal and energy with which you have served it in all circumstances. Recently, moreover, since it has pleased divine providence to call our poor unworthy selves to the summit of the apostolic office, your light has shone with ever increasing brightness, whilst your unfailing fidelity and devotion have become known not only to those around you but even to far distant nations. No fatigue, no threats, no flattery could prevent you from standing like an impregnable fortress against the tyranny of Peter Pierleone or from working to win over the King and the other princes to the obedience of Saint Peter. It is right, therefore, that the Apostolic See, which rejoices so greatly to have such a devoted son, should pay its debt of gratitude to you for all your services and labours and thus bind you even more closely to its service». The bull then went on to grant Norbert the confirmation for which he had previously asked of the metropolitan jurisdiction of the see of Magdeburg over all the bishops of Pomerania and Poland.

While the army was still in Rome one of the soldiers was suddenly struck down by such a serious and apparently inexplicable illness that he was thought to be possessed by an evil spirit. His comrades took him to the Pope, demanding that he should cure him, but Innocent took offence at their disrespectful manner and went away into his private apartments, leaving the sick man in the church, where Norbert was with a few others. He was grieved to see the man's condition and said to his companions : «Let us turn to the Lord in a humble and contrite spirit, asking Him to take pity on this poor fellow». Then he began to pray silently and remained in prayer from midday until the evening when, after a violent paroxysm, the sick man fell asleep and after a short while woke up completely cured. Norbert advised him to go to confession and to abstain from all rich foods for a period for fear of a relapse, which he agreed to do. All went well until they came to Pisa on the homeward march when, forgetful of his promises, the man broke out and indulged himself freely. Once more he was afflicted by the same terrible sufferings as before and Norbert had to be called in again to restore him to health.

Before leaving Rome Lothar made one last effort to end the schism, sending Norbert and Bernard of Clairvaux to Anacletus, but to no avail as the anti-pope remained obdurate. He held all the strong points in the City and knew that the imperial army was too weak to dislodge him.

Lothar set out on his return journey during the first half of June and by 19 July he had crossed the Appenines and was in the territory of Parma; by 30 July he was at Campo Leonardo, near Mantua. The only opposition that the army met was near Brescia, where a local landowner tried to bar its approach to the Alps, but he was defeated without difficulty and was taken prisoner.

On 23 August the Emperor was at Freising, North of Munich, and on 5 September he made his triumphal entry into Würzburg, where he held a diet three days later. At this Adalbero, Abbot of Nienburg, was appointed Bishop of Basle, probably on the recommendation of Norbert, whom he had accompanied to Rome. In the course of a discussion which now arose Norbert supported the claim that the approval of the leaders of the laity, which in his view included the Emperor and other rulers, should be sought before the confirmation of a bishop's election. In this he departed from the extreme views of many of the reformers. Whilst he was never willing to compromise on a matter of principle, he always followed a realistic policy and was ready to make legitimate concessions when useful results might be expected. Ever unswerving in his absolute loyalty to the Church, he yet had a sympathetic understanding of the difficulties and problems of civil rulers. His task in keeping the peace between Church and State was far from easy and it called for all his tact and diplomatic skill, for Lothar was not always so pious and amenable as he is usually depicted to have been.

From Würzburg Norbert went with the Emperor to Mainz, where another diet was held on 18 October, and thence to Basle on 8 November and down the Rhine to Cologne for Christmas. The Court was at Aachen for the Epiphany and at Goslar on 25 January but by February Norbert's health had broken down completely so that not even his indomitable spirit could force his enfeebled body to carry on. His naturally strong constitution had been undermined by many years of extreme austerity, continuous overwork and frequent travel over bad roads in all kinds of weather, even before the summer climate of Italy, and probably malaria, had taken their toll of his strength.

It had been his wish to get back to his diocese immediately on his return to Germany but Lothar had been unwilling to part with him and had kept him at court acting as Arch-Chancellor of the Empire. Now he was seriously ill and had to take to his bed, which he was seldom to leave in the four months of life that remained to him. Slowly and painfully he was carried back to Magdeburg where he arrived by Ash Wednesday, which fell on 28 February in 1134. He continued to administer the diocese from his sick bed, although he was in constant pain. He could still get up and walk a little without help and during Lent he spent some time at the Abbey of Bergen in the suburbs as well as visiting his brethren at Saint Mary's. There was a great deal that he had wished to do during his episcopate such as installing his brethren as the cathedral chapter and completing the buildings which had been planned by Otto the Great but he had never had the time. He did however have the satisfaction at this time of bringing to a successful conclusion a matter of great delicacy which had been at issue ever since he became archbishop. Frederick, the younger son of the Count Palatine, had been destined by his parents for a career in the Curch and had been placed by them as a canon of the Cathedral Chapter of Magdeburg when he was little more than a child. When his elder brother died in 1125 his mother abducted him by stealth and betrothed him to the daughter of a count. Although he was only fourteen at the time the boy remained firm in his resolve to follow his vocation and secretly sent word of his situation to Norbert, who did all that he could to secure his return but apparently achieved nothing. At last with Lothar's support, he succeeded in persuading the mother to release her son, by now a young man of twenty five, and he came back to Magdeburg where he was in due course ordained priest.

By an almost superhuman effect Norbert went to the cathedral on Maundy Thursday to bless the Holy Oils and again on Easter Sunday, 15 April, when, seated in a chair, he celebrated the High Mass, which was to be his last Mass.

His illness was getting worse and it must have been quite clear by now that there was no possibility of his recovery but Norbert remained calm and serene in his perfect acceptance of God's will. He still attended to the affairs of the diocese and of his Order, and now he sent for Conrad of Querfurt, a canon of the Cathedral who, it will be remembered, had been elected before Norbert but had been debarred from becoming archbishop because he was only a subdeacon. He spoke to him in confidence about the probability that he would be his successor and, among other things, commended to his care and protection the young community of Gottesgnaden, asking him to grant it a charter confirming in due legal form all that he had done there.

Often during his last illness Norbert had the religious of Saint Mary's assembled round his bed so that he could talk to them. He also sent to Prémontré for Hugh to come to him but the latter put off his departure so as to attend to some business, not realizing the urgency of the summons, and so he arrived too late to find Norbert still alive. His beloved Evermode, however, remained with him to the end, caring for him and hardly ever leaving his side.

Norbert received Holy Communion very frequently and on Whit Sunday, 3 June, knowing that the end was near he asked for and received with great devotion the Annointing of the Sick. On the Tuesday he took a turn for the worse and a message was sent to the community of Saint Mary's to come at once. He continued to sink during the night but remained in full possession of his faculties to the last. He gave his final blessing to his religious brethren and to the rest of the clergy who were present and, with the name of Christ on his lips, he passed away peacefully. It was 6 June 1134, nineteen years since his conversion, fourteen years since he founded Prémontré and almost deight years since he became archbishop.

CHAPTER XVIII

BURIAL AND CANONISATION.

When it came to making the funeral arrangements there was a disagreement over the place of burial. The Cathedral Chapter claimed that as Archbishop he must be buried in his own metropolitan cathedral, whilst the community of Saint Mary's argued that his body should rest among his own religious brethren, whose father and superior he had been to the end. Moreover he himself had more than once expressly stated his wish to be buried among them. Since there was no possibility of reaching an agreement, the matter was referred to the Emperor, who happened to be at Merseburg, about sixty miles away, where a deputation from the Cathedral Chapter and the representatives of Saint Mary's led by Evermode went to him. Having heard all the arguments from each side, he had no hesitation in deciding that Norbert's body should rest with his own religious family.

Each day between his death and burial Norbert's body lay in state in one or other of the city churches, where the Vigil of the Dead and a requiem Mass were celebrated. It was remarked at the time that the body remained completely incorrupt, although the weather was exceptionally hot, even for midsummer.

The funeral took place on 11 June and the body was buried in the nave of Saint Mary's in front of the altar of the Holy Cross which stood at the entrance to the choir, but a few years later it was moved into the choir so as to be nearer to the brethren.

On the night that Norbert died a brother at Prémontré, who was sleeping in one of the granges belonging to the abbey, had a dream in which he saw him clothed in white, with an olive branch in his hand. Surprised, he asked whence he came and whither he was going and received the reply : «I have been sent from Heaven with this olive branch and I am going with all speed to plant it at Prémontré, the place of my poverty». As soon as he was awake the brother went to the monastery and told several of his confreres about his dream. It made such an impression on them that they made a note of the date and time of the apparition and, when at length the news of Norbert's death came, it was found that it had taken place on that very night.

Then one of the priests in the abbey dreamt that Norbert was standing in front of him. Suddenly he became transformed and in his place he saw a lily of surpassing beauty which the angels plucked and carried away to heaven. When he woke at dawn he hurried at once to the Prior to ask permission to say mass for the repose of the soul of their father, Norbert. The prior asked the reason for his request and, when he heard it, he told him to remember the date which they later learnt was that of the funeral.

No one at Prémontré felt the loss of their father and founder more than Hugh, who had been his close friend and confidant for so many years. His grief was all the harder to bear because he was troubled by doubts about his friend's salvation. He prayed earnestly to be given some assurance in the matter and then, one night in a dream, he found himself in a magnificent palace with his beloved master. He threw himself on his knees and begged him to tell him about his present state. Norbert raised him up, embraced him affectionately and invited him to sit with him. He told Hugh that God had called him to Himself and that now he was at rest and enjoyed perfect peace. There was still one thing that Hugh wanted to ask him. Had he taken it ill that he had not come when he sent for him before his death ? «You will come one day», Norbert replied and then disappeared, leaving Hugh consoled and comforted.

It was to be four and a half centuries before Norbert was canonised, although Saint Bernard of Clairvaux, who died in 1153, was canonised only twenty one years after his death. The reason for this long delay was the failure of the Order to promote his cause, which may have arisen in part out of a disagreement between Prémontré and Magdeburg. A record of the many miracles claimed to have been worked at his tomb was kept but it perished together with some of Norbert's writings in the great fire which destroyed Saint Mary's and a large part of the city in 1193. It was reconstructed from memory as far as possible by the community, who presented it to Innocent III in 1200 with a view to obtaining their founder's canonisation but their efforts seem to have been fruitless. In 1521 the General Chapter of the Order decided to reintroduce the cause and appointed Nicholas Psaume, Abbot of Saint Paul's at Verdun, to act as Postulator. He visited the libraries of Rome, where he found some record of earlier proceedings and several martyrologies that included Norbert's name, but no further progress was made and it was another sixty years before anything more was done. Then the Abbot General, Jean Despruets, with the support of the Cardinal Protector of the Order, approached the Pope. A search was made in the archives of the Roman Church and an ancient manuscript was found which contained all the evidence that was necessary to prove the heroic sanctity of Norbert. So much work had already been done that it was possible to by-pass the lengthy procedures generally required and so at last on 28 July 1582 Gregory XIII promulgated the bull formally canonising Norbert.

There was still one thing lacking – the shrine of the new saint. His tomb was now in the possession of the Lutherans, who had expelled the White Canons from Saint Mary's at Magdeburg in 1540. Over the next 44 years frequent attempts were made to recover the saint's body but it was not until December 1626 that the Abbot of Strahov in Prague was successful.

When he opened the tomb he found the skeleton intact with each bone in place and complete sets of teeth in both the lower and upper jaws. Except for the gold embroidered borders and the metal clasp the material of the vestments had perished.

The body was taken to Prague and was solemnly enshrined in the abbey church of Strahov, where it rests to this days. Alas ! the abbey has been suppressed by the communists; the last abbot died in prison for the Faith and the community have all been dispersed, whilst the abbey church is a Museum of Atheism !

What matters most, however, is not where Norbert's mortal remains rest but that his spirit and ideals are still alive and flourishing wherever his spiritual childen live and work throughout the world.

EPILOGUE

SAINT NORBERT'S LEGACY : HIS ORDER IN THE WORLD TODAY.

There are some saints of whom little more is remembered than their names but there are others who have continued to exert a powerful influence in the Church down the ages and among these are to be counted the founders of religious orders.

A study of the life of Saint Norbert shows him to have been very much a man of his own times but the more deeply one reflects on it, the more relevant his message is seen to be in our day.

In the 12th century a number of orders of canons regular came into existence and some flourished exceedingly. Why is it then that while most of them have disappeared the Order of Prémontré, in spite of disasters which at one time well nigh extinguished it, still plays a not inconsiderable part in the life of the Church today ? It has remained true to its founder's ideals and has possessed a flexibility that has enabled it to meet changing circumstances. Even in its earliest years when most foundations were in solitary places like Prémontré Norbert made some in cities like Saint Michael's at Antwerp and Saint Martin's at Laon, whilst his houses in the province of Magdeburg were centres of missionary activity.

Quite early in the history of the Order two important

changes took place. In 1140, just six years after Saint Norbert's death, it was decided that double monasteries were undesirable and so the convents of sisters were moved some distance away from the abbeys. The sisters now became canonesses, leading a purely contemplative life and supporting the apostolate of the canons by their prayers. At the same time there was a falling off in the numbers of laybrothers so that by about the year 1230 they had almost entirely disappeared. Meanwhile many country parishes had been established and entrusted to the Order.

During the Middle Ages the Order spread to every part of Christendom and the total number of abbeys rose to about 650. There were 30 in England (none very large) and 3 priories of nuns, 1 in Wales and 5 and a cathedral priory in Scotland, whilst Ireland had 4 abbeys and 7 priories (2 or 3 of which were of nuns).

Then in the 16th century came the Protestant Reformation which brought about the dissolution of all the houses of the Order in the British Isles, Scandinavia and those parts of Germany which adopted the new religion so that by the year 1572 there were only 197 abbeys left including 99 in France. The final disaster came with the French Revolution and the wars that followed it which led to the suppression of all the houses in France and in the countries occupied by Napoleon's armies, except those in Spain, and even these did not survive long, being closed by an anticlerical government in 1833. Thus all that was left of the Order was a few abbeys in the Austrian Empire. Indeed it looked as though it was doomed to extinction but the 19th century saw a wonderful revival which began when the surviving canons restored the great abbeys in Belgium and Holland and through them the Order returned to England and was established in the U.S.A. The

20th century has seen a remarkable growth but sadly the abbeys in Hungary and Czechoslovakia were suppressed by the communist governments after World War II.

The Order consists of autonomous communities (or canonries) and, unlike those of later orders, the religious are professed for a particular community. Normally a canonry is governed by an abbot but there are also autonomous priories which have not yet become abbeys. The supreme authority in the Order is the General Chapter which is presided over by the Abbot General and consists of the superiors of all houses and delegates elected by the communities as well as the officials of the Order. It meets every six years and when it is not in session the Order is governed by the Abbot General with the assistance of a council of four definitors elected by the General Chapter.

The Order is divided into circaries (12), groups of all the houses speaking the same language, whose function it is to promote the unity of the Order and to ensure that all the directives and instructions of the General Chapter are put into effect. The Vicar of the Abbot General is the link between the central government of the Order and the houses of the circary.

Like all other orders the Order was reformed as a result

(12) Originally the abbot of the mother house carried out the visitation of all the houses founded from it but this proved excessively burdensome for the abbots of older abbeys with many daughter houses and also it was difficult where the two houses were at a distance from each other or separated by the boundaries of hostile states. To meet this situation the Order devised a system of circaries each covering a certain area for purposes of visitation. Thus England and Scotland were divided into three circaries North, Central and South. Now the visitors are appointed by the General Chapter and the circaries are as described in the text.

of Vatican II but, unlike certain previous reforms which were concerned with the restoration of primitive or mediaeval practices and observances, this reform has been an attempt to return to the inspiration and ideals of the founder and to apply them in terms of present day life.

Saint Norbert summed up his ideal as «to follow the sacred scriptures and to have Christ as leader». This meant to live according to the Gospel and the way of life of the Apostles which was summarized in the Rule of Saint Augustine and which is now applied to present day conditions by the Constitutions of the Order. The Norbertine, like the Apostles, answers Christ's call to leave all things and follow Him. He sees as the pattern of all religious communities Christ living with the Apostles, forming them by His teaching and example, and also sending them out to proclaim the coming of the Kingdom of God. Then, after Pentecost, we find the first christians gathered round the Apostles, having all things in common. As we have seen already this was the model for all the communities of canons regular.

At the beginning of his Rule Saint Augustine says : «The first purpose for which you have come together is to live in unity in the house and to be of one mind and one heart in God». Life under the Rule is community life and those who live under it give not only their goods but also themselves to the community. There is no room for a «loner» in the Order.

If there was a special virtue which Saint Norbert stressed it was love when he quoted the Rule to the brethren : «let us love God above all things, then our neighbour». A Norbertine community can never be inward looking; it must be inspired by a zeal for souls which draws its priests out into the world, like Saint Norbert, to work for the sanctification of their neighbours, whilst the community welcomes the faithful to assist at their Divine Office and Mass and receives groups of all kinds as well as individuals who come to make retreats or for spiritual refreshment.

The first duty of any canon regular is the public celebration with the greatest possible solemnity of the Church's prayer, the Divine Office, with the community Mass as its summit up to which everything else leads and from which everything else flows. Private prayer, meditation, spiritual reading and especially familiarity with the Scriptures are essential. All pastoral activity and priestly ministry are the overflow and outward expression of the life of prayer and union with God.

At his profession the Norbertine promises «a conversion of my ways», a continual effort at self-reform, to grow daily more like Christ. «He must increase, I must decrease.» Augustine and Norbert both took to heart these words of John the Baptist.

The Church and the tradition of the Order exhort us to a life of penance. This does not mean so much external penances as the daily taking up of one's cross – all the trials, troubles, difficulties and sufferings of life borne willingly for the love of God. As to fasting and abstinence the law of the Church and local custom are followed.

The Order has two special devotions – to the Humanity of Our Lord, particularly in the Blessed Sacrament of the Altar, and to Our Blessed Lady, Queen and Mother of the Order, especially in her Immaculate Conception and her Assumption and as the channel of all graces.

The Order is not specialized like many later orders and congregations but is prepared for any and every kind of priestly work – as parish clergy, as missionaries, teaching in schools, colleges and seminaries, giving retreats, as chaplains to universities, schools and convents, in the apostolate of groups of all kinds and at centres of pilgrimage.

In particular there is the spiritual formation and direction of the members of the Third Order, lay people who share the spirit of the Order and are affiliated to a canonry in whose life and work they try to share. Secular priests can also join the Third Order or become associated with the Order in other ways.

To conclude, in this nuclear age when the world's greatest need is for peace who could be a better patron for those who work and pray for it than Saint Norbert who was such an outstanding apostle of reconciliation and peace ?

THE PRESENT STATE OF THE ORDER

The total membership of the Order as at 1 January, 1983, was 1,558 – that is 1,355 priests and brothers and 203 nuns in 7 priories (2 each in Belgium, Poland and Spain and 1 in France).

In addition there are congregations of sisters engaged in active work (formerly known as the Third Order Regular) in Switzerland, Austria, Germany, Czechoslovakia and Hungary.

All the members of the **Bohemian** (or Czech) and **Hungarian Circaries,** having been expelled from their monasteries by the communists, at present live dispersed.

The main strength of the Order has long been in the **Circary of Brabant** (Flemish speaking Belgium and the Netherlands). It numbers 599 priests and brothers in its 6 ancient abbeys.

The **French Speaking Circary** with 90 members has 2 abbeys in France and 1 in Belgium.

The **German Speaking Circary** (Austria and Germany), 181 strong, has 4 abbeys and 3 independent priories.

The **English Speaking Circary**, 345 strong, includes the following : –

Daylesford Abbey in Pennsylvania, U.S.A., with 66 professed and 3 novices has 2 dependent priories and 2 secondary schools.

De Pere Abbey in Wisconsin, U.S.A., with 116 professed and 9 novices, has 2 dependent priories and a house of studies in Chicago as well as 1 college and 2 high schools.

It also has a mission at Lima in Peru where it has founded a dependent house.

Orange Abbey in California, U.S.A., with 24 professed and 8 postulants, was founded in 1961 for those of the community of the Abbey of Csorna in Hungary who had been able to come to the U.S.A. but since 1966 it has received American subjects. It has a dependent house, The Norbertine Faculty House, Santa Ana, and a number of the priests teach in the neighbouring preparatory high school.

Jamtara Priory at Jabalpur in India has 53 professed, 11 novices and 13 postulants. It has 4 dependent communities and a high school in Bombay.

Kilnacrott Abbey in Co. Cavan, Ireland, with 32 professed and 5 novices has a priory in Western Australia with its own novitiate and also a secondary school. The abbey has also made a foundation in Scotland but there is not yet a formed house.

Storrington Priory with 9 priests (plus 2 attached from Kilnacrott) has a dependent house in Manchester. It is dedicated to Our Lady of England and is a centre of pilgrimage.

There are 2 independent priories that do not belong to any circary, namely

Saint Constant in the Province of Quebec, Canada, with 11 professed and 2 novices and

Jau in Brazil with 19 professed and 6 novices.

There is a quasi-independent priory at Kinshasa in Zaire with 23 professed and 13 novices.

Various abbeys have dependent houses in Brazil, Chile and the Cape Province of South Africa and missions in Denmark, India and Zaire.

All the canonries have some parishes entrusted to them.

Further information about the Order can be obtained by writing to any of the following addresses :

Rt. Rev. Father Abbot, O.Praem.,
St. Norbert Abbey,
1016 North Broadway,
De Pere, Wisconsin 54115, U.S.A.

Rt. Rev. Father Abbot, O.Praem.
Kilnacrott Abbey,
Ballyjamesduff,
Co. Cavan, Ireland

Rt. Rev. Father Prior, O.Praem.,
Our Lady of England Priory,
Storrington, Pulborough,
West Sussex, RH20 4LN, England

APPENDIX A

THE DATE AND PLACE OF BIRTH AND FAMILY OF SAINT NORBERT

In the Middle Ages people did not take the same interest as we do in the family background and early formative years of the saints and in the case of Saint Norbert his early biographers tell us very little about his life before his conversion. In their view these were wasted years and any account of them would have had little or no spiritual value.

YEAR OF BIRTH. Even the year of his birth is uncertain. We know that he was ordained priest in 1115, for which the minimum canonical age was then thirty. Moreover we read that the archbishop was surprised by his request for ordination because he had declined it several times in the past when it was offered to him. He had also refused the bishopric of Cambrai, which had fallen vacant in June 1113 and which the Emperor had wished him to accept. These facts would suggest that Norbert had attained the age of thirty some time before June 1113.

Vita «A» describes him as being «in the full vigour of middle life» in 1115 but in November 1118 he was still able to speak of «his youth» to Pope Gelasius II, which would hardly be consistent with his being much, if at all, over thirty five then.

We can, therefore, with reasonable certainty put the year of his birth before 1085 but how much before we cannot say. We know that he was enrolled in the collegiate chapter at Xanten during the provostship of Adalger, who died in 1089, and we are also told that he was a canon there «almost from his infancy» (ferme ab infantia) from which we might infer that he was born no later than 1083. Abbot Hugo put his birth in 1080, a year that has been commonly accepted by later writers including Père Petit. It is a convenient round number and is certainly the earliest date that has any evidence to support it. We can reasonably place Saint Norbert's birth as not earlier than 1080 and before the middle of 1083.

PLACE OF BIRTH. The early biographers make no mention of the place of Norbert's birth. This honour has been claimed for Xanten on the strength of the statements of these biographers that «he became well known in the town of Xanten» (Vita «A». Claruit in municipio Sanctensi) and that «there lived in the year 1115 a certain Norbert, a German by birth, from the town of Xanten» (Vita «B». Fuit anno 1115 vir quidam Norbertus, natione Teutonicus, municipio de Sanctis). These mean no more than that Norbert was living in Xanten in 1115. It is true that there is a tradition in Xanten that he was born there which can be traced back at least to the year 1700 and that a house, 27 Marsstrasse, has been shown as his birthplace.

On the other hand the main family seat from which the family took its name was at Gennep and it might be expected that it was there that they mostly resided.

A claim has also been made for Torneche, near Wesel, on the Rhine solely on the ground that Norbert had some property there but this claim can certainly be rejected out of hand.

Abbot Hugo and Madelaine both support the claim of Xanten but it makes little difference which was his actual birthplace; there is do doubt about the district in which he was born. It was at Xanten that he was educated; throughout his life he was known as Norbert of Xanten and he always retained a special affection for the place.

FAMILY. All that his biographers tell us of Norbert's ancestry is that he was German and came of a noble family descended from the Franks and the Salian Germans. We also know that his mother had some influential relatives living in the neighbourhood of Laon. There is no support in the early sources for the assertions of some later writers that he was descended through his father from the emperors of the Salian dynasty and through his mother from the Dukes of Lorraine.

The Franks were a group of Germanic tribes which, when we first come across them, were living on the borders of the Roman Empire along the East bank of the Rhine. In the middle of the 4th Century one branch the Salian Franks, moved into the Empire, occupying the present day Brabant and becoming vassal allies of the Romans (Foederati). By the end of the 5th century the Franks were consolidated in two main groups – the Salian Franks in the present day Flanders and Brabant and the Ripuarian Franks on the middle Rhine around Cologne. Even after the conquest of Roman Gaul by the Franks some of them remained in their homelands. Gennep, of which Norbert's familiy were the lords was thus in the ancestral territory of the Salian Franks and we know that he was of aristocratic descent. Moreover throughout his life he seems to have been accepted as an equal by members of the highest nobility.

APPENDIX B

THE THIRD ORDER

It is certain that Saint Norbert did not write a rule for tertiaries – he did not do this even for the canons – nor did he give Count Theobald a small scapular to wear under his outer garments for these small scapulars did not come into use until more than a century later. Moreover Père Petit tells us that Count Theobald was not associated with the White Canons in any exclusive way for he was buried in a Cistercian abbey wearing the Cistercian habit.

During the Middle Ages there was a great desire among lay people to be associated with the monks and canons so as to have some share in their masses and prayers during life and especially after death. So it became customary as early as the beginning of the 9th century for Benedictine abbeys to receive benefactors into confraternity. The «confrater» untertook no specific obligation but was given a special share in the masses and prayers of the community to which he was affiliated. (This kind of confraternity still exists in some of the English Benedictine abbeys).

There were those, however, who aspired after more than this and desired to end their lives in the security of the monastic state. This led to a custom, which became common between the 10th and 13th centuries but ultimately passed away, of clothing lay people as well as bishops and secular priests with the monastic habit during their last illness. Apparently they made some form of profession because it seems that, if they recovered, they remained bound to the monastic life. Such people were said to be received «ad succurrendum» (i.e. for the help that they would receive as members of a religious community).

Both these practices, which were universal among the Benedictines and also existed among the Augustinian Canons, were taken over by the White Canons and there are many records of the grants of confraternity and of the reception of brothers and sisters «ad succurendum».

It is possible that «frater (or soror) ad succurrendum» did not have the same meaning at all times and in all places. It may even be that some of those who were received into «fraternity» and granted a share in the masses, prayers and good works of the Order were described as brothers and sisters «ad succurrendum». It would also be natural for them in their desire to be more closely associated with the Order to adopt a way of life based as far as their circumstances allowed on that of the canons.

There is no record of the existence of the Third Order earlier than the 17th century when in 1633 J. Le Paige in his «Bibliotheca ordinis Praemonstratensis» asserts that Saint Norbert, wishing to provide a more religious way of life for those living in the world, drew up some rules for Count Theobald and gave him a small white scapular, and he says that many in all ranks of society followed the Count's example. Le Paige tells us that the Rule formerly prescribed an office consisting of the Creed and a large number of Our Fathers and Hail Marys; confession and communion 7 times a year; and fasting every Friday. He also gives the ritual in use in his day for conferring the scapular and says that the name of the new «brother ad succerrendum» is to be entered in the register. In 1704 in his «Life of Saint Norbert» Abbot Hugo writes of the institution of the Third Order by the saint as an unquestionable fact and subsequent writers, whether members of the Order or not, have made the same assumption and have credited Saint Norbert with having conceived the notion of a third order as a way of enabling lay people living in the world to share in the benefits of the religious life. In 1751 the White Canons in Bavaria obtained papal approval of a revised Rule for their tertiaries to replace an old one no longer adapted to the needs of their time.

Thus it is evident that five centuries after Saint Norbert's death the Third Order as we know it today had already existed from time immemorial but how and when it had developed we do not know. Today the Order of Prémontré is the only order in the Church apart from the friars to have a Third Order properly so-called.